# LIFE CHANGING CHOICES

## The 7 Essential Choices at the Heart of Transformational Change for Foster Youth and Your Community

## About
# Just in Time for Foster Youth

*Just in Time for Foster Youth's mission is to engage a caring community to help transition age foster youth become Confident, Capable, and Connected and achieve self-sufficiency, well-being, and life satisfaction.*

*We believe access to critical resources and consistent long-term positive connections are the foundations for the success of the youth we serve so they can thrive and enjoy productive, satisfying lives and break the cycle of foster care.*

*We envision a future in which every youth leaving the foster care system has a reliable, responsive, and real community of caring adults and supportive peers waiting for them after 18.*

ISBN 979-8-9875699-1-7

**Just in Time for Foster Youth**
4560 Alvarado Canyon. 2G
San Diego CA.  92120
619-269-5422
jitfosteryouth.org
Tax ID # 20-5448416

*Cover design by Don Ulinski*
*Back cover photo by Carol Sonstein*

*This book is dedicated to*
*all the amazing Young People*
*in our Just in Time Community*
*and everyone in our Extended Family*
*who help provide access to*
*a World of Life Changing Choices*

Proceeds from the sale of book will be used share the Just in Time mission with other organizations across the nation.

# CONTENTS

## Why We Wrote This 8
***Nyla's* Story** *"No Role Models and I'm Here Right Now"*

## PART 1
## The System Is NOT Broken 15
***Tasha's* Story** *"Enough Courage to Raise My Hand"*

San Diego, We Have a Problem...and It's Not New 19
Origins & Inevitable Failures of the Foster Care System 21
These are OUR Children: The Early Years of Just in Time 29
Why are You Still Here? The "Biggest Gap" 31
Building Reliable, Responsive, Real Community 33
Life Changing Choices 39

## PART 2

## The 7 Essential Choices 45

*Zane's Story "New Memories in a World of My Own Making"*

**CHOICE ONE**: What's Your Intention? 49
*Prioritize Protection or Empowerment*

**CHOICE TWO:** Who are You Serving? 59
*See Damaged & Broken or Creative, Resourceful, & Whole*

**CHOICE THREE:** What will You Promise? 79
*Build a System or a Community*

**CHOICE FOUR***:* Where will You Find Answers? 97
*Act from YOUR Agenda or Listen to Lived Experience Experts*

**CHOICE FIVE:** When will You Know You're Succeeding? 113
*Report What was Done or Share What had Lasting Impact*

**CHOICE SIX:** How will You Sustain Your Efforts? 135
*Follow the Funding or Engage with Impact*

**CHOICE SEVEN**: Who can Start THIS Where You Live? 157
*Wait for Someone Else or Be the Needed Change*

## PART 3

## The Choice to Fail Our Children 173

*Victoria's Story "The Family I Always Dreamed Of"*

## Appendix & Takeaways 185

Diane    Don    Irving

James    Nathaniel    Simone

# Why We Wrote This

Caitlin    Zane    Nyla

Tasha    Vanessa    Victoria

## "No Role Models and I'm Here Right Now"
# Nyla's Story

*I was permanently placed in the foster care system at 13 years old with my three younger sisters. We were put into foster care due to the physical, emotional and sexual abuse we experienced from our mom and her boyfriends.*

*Growing up with unsafe and unstable adults made me believe I was incapable of achieving my dreams. I was afraid I was also going to end up a drug addict like the adults around me or I was going to take my own life by the time I was 15 years old.*

*My sisters were my motivation to create a healthy and fulfilling life for us, despite not having the role models I needed. Unfortunately, we were soon separated when my stepdad got custody of all three sisters while I stayed in foster care.*

*Although it was so hard for me to know I couldn't protect my sisters, I pushed myself to get good grades and go to college, hoping that foster care would support me in achieving my goals. But when I expressed my desire to attend a private university, I was met with discouragement and dismissal.*

*After my stepdad moved to Arizona with my sisters, I knew he was going to hurt them more and I ended up falling into a deep depression. I was afraid I wouldn't be able make positive changes for my sisters and me after all. I tried my best to keep in contact with them and there wasn't a day that went by that I didn't beg to be reunited with them. I made sure I did everything I could in my present day to keep making the positive changes I believed we deserved.*

I did make it to college but, without role models, I continued to struggle. I was surrounded by those who doubted my ability to overcome my trauma and achieve my dreams. I had to become my own role model, pushing myself to persevere even when I doubted I could succeed. But to be real- I also cried many times. I longed to have people in my life who would support me unconditionally.

It was when I moved to San Diego during college that everything began to change for me. This was when I connected with Just in Time.

Need books for school? JIT was there. When I was ready to get my driver's license, JIT had me covered with Changing Lanes. In College Bound, I received a laptop, a printer, and furnishings. Every JIT service provided me with one more building block on my pathway to success.

And through the unconditional support I've received from people like Reshae, Sanam, Esmeralda, Diane, Don and so many others, I've learned about my strengths and have a better understanding of my unique capabilities. I have JIT to thank for all of that.

Most importantly, I've been connected to the greatest coaches who are my mentors. Not only do they understand me; they accept me into their homes and families with open arms. And thanks to this support, I've grown into being a person who fully believes in myself.

Earlier this year, I was able to gain custody of one of my sisters, and she is thriving! I'm also proud to say that, not only did I graduate from my dream university, I'm also the first person in my family to get her master's degree.

After being told by others for so long that I was not a leader or qualified to help students in higher education, I'm Student Advisor at Alliant University, assisting Psychology students with attaining their PhD.

But all of this is just the beginning of my success. I'm striving to work in the mental health field, helping others to heal their traumas and reach their full potential. Because Just in Time has cared for me and empowered me in so many ways, I'm no longer fearful of the unknown or afraid to face my fears.

When I look back at my life, I resonate so much with J. Cole's lyrics, "No role models and I'm here right now," because despite growing up with "no role models," I'm here right now and I have a community who has my back and supports me to be the best version of myself every day, and that's Just in Time for Foster Youth. - **Nyla**

# Nyla is why we wrote this.

And Aaron and Amanda. Nancy and Nathaniel. Isaac and Ivana. Jessica, Johnny, Makayla and Mario. Raul, Rebekkah, Steven and Stephany. Tasha and Thomas. Vivian and Victor and hundreds of other young people who left the foster care system over the years and joined our Just in Time for Foster Youth (JIT) Community as partners in their own success and well-being.

We wrote this book to begin a conversation about a bold new idea - or maybe to resurrect a forgotten fundamental truth - that might just break the cycle of foster care.

**Children and families thrive in communities, not systems.**

After all the resources and effort dedicated to improving child welfare systems, with little significant change in positive outcomes, we invite exploration of an alternative. A different approach to resources for children and families struggling to thrive that might ultimately replace what isn't working today.

We wrote this book because we've continued to see a stubborn truth over the last two decades about the critical necessity of **Community** and **Connection**. A truth reinforced by history and our own experience about why systems will resist change and are unlikely to be empowering, healthy places for young people or families, despite our best intentions.

This book is not a lecture but a challenge for all of us to consider a different point of view. A mindset and model that has empowered our efforts at Just in Time and might do the same for people in <u>any</u> community who are frustrated by the persistent trauma that seems built into the current experience of our children in care.

*And we believe that <u>all</u> the young people impacted by foster care are <u>our</u> children.*

We wrote this book so you can hear their voices, as we have. So that you can get to know their stories as we have.

Once you do, we hope you seek out their stories in <u>your</u> community and ask others to join and listen.

Most of all, we want this book to start your own crucial conversations about the old Assumptions and the Choices we <u>can</u> change, replacing historically negative outcomes with lasting positive Empowerment.

## That's why we wrote this book.
## So we can do this together now.

Caitlin Radigan
> *Key Partnerships Manager*

Diane Cox
> *Chief Sustainability Officer*

Don Wells
> *Chief Empowerment Officer*

Irving Chavez
> *Chief Impact Officer*

James Hidds-Monroe
> *Impact and Systems Data Strategist*

Nathaniel Martinez
> *Managing Coordinator, Financial Fitness*

Simone Hidds-Monroe
> *Chief Advocacy & Community Empowerment Officer*

Vanessa Davis
> *Chief Visionary, Rise & Thrive*

**Join the Life Changing Movement at
jitfosteryouth.org/100KCommunity**

Nyla & her JIT Coach

# Part 1

# The System
# Is <u>NOT</u> Broken

## *"Enough Courage to Raise My Hand"*
# Tasha's Story

*I was placed in the foster care system as a baby with no choice in the matter. While my foster parents provided my basic needs, they were physically, mentally, and emotionally abusive. They would say I was "mentally retarded" because I was diagnosed with cerebral palsy, developmental disabilities, and visual impairment due to high myopia.*

*Most of the time I was quiet because I feared major physical disciplinary actions. I remember feeling so much shame when I was punished for teasing my brother. I was forced to hold my hands high up in the air for three hours. If I lowered them, I'd get whipped. I wasn't allowed to speak for myself when social workers were present.*

*The only place I could break out of my shell was at school. I had just enough courage to raise my hand and answer questions in class. This is where I began realizing my potential.*

*I graduated from high school with a 4.3 GPA and was accepted to multiple universities, including UC Berkeley and UC San Diego. Through College Bound, Just in Time provided me with a laptop, printer, dorm supplies, and a mentor.*

*I was off to UC Berkeley but soon found myself struggling, so I returned to my foster home where my foster parents had this "I knew you couldn't do it" attitude. I was able to transfer to UC San Diego, but my foster parents took full control of my life.*

16

Fortunately, Just in Time staff were there during this difficult time; they believed in me when I barely believed in myself. So, by the end of my freshman year, I had found the courage to move on-campus.

Unfortunately, my foster parents took advantage of me financially and committed fraud by cashing my Extended Foster Care checks every month while I was away at school. They stole about $10,000 and never had to pay it back. They blamed me for speaking up to the social worker and shut me out of their lives.

Because of these traumas, I was hospitalized and academically disqualified. I felt disillusioned, betrayed, and exhausted from all the crying over the loss of the only family I knew.

Slowly, I found my way back from hardship and loss to health and connection. I was able to forgive my foster family, re-connect with my biological family, attend church, and build friendships. I graduated with a degree in Ethnic Studies and a minor in Literature/Writing.

Throughout this challenging period of my life, Just in Time was there for me, bringing a cushion of knowledge, support, and healing to my journey of finding my path. I received help with managing my finances, exploring career paths, public speaking, and connecting with amazing coaches on my journey to success.

I'm still healing and learning what it means for my voice to be heard. I've advocated for foster youth in San Diego, Washington, D.C. and globally. And, in a few months, I will have a master's degree in Social Innovation from the University of San Diego.

*I care deeply about being a voice for the voiceless and giving agency to those who feel less empowered to speak and be heard. I know who I am and where I'm going, and I'm learning about the redemptive, loving power of sharing my story so other youth just like me can rise up.* **- Tasha**

# San Diego, We Have a Problem...

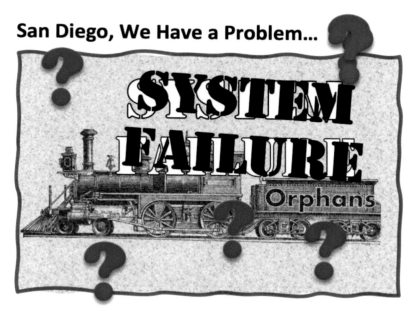

SYSTEM FAILURE

Orphans

## ...and It's Not New

# Let's talk about **The System.**

So where do we start?  At this moment, there are about 400,000 foster youth in the child welfare system nationwide and the number of children touched by foster care is increasing.

This, despite efforts to have <u>fewer</u> children removed from their parents and homes to enter foster care. There are signs that a host of factors – including economic insecurity, opioid addiction, mental health challenges, and the pandemic – are <u>increasing</u> the number of children and young adults impacted by foster care. *(Scientific American)*

**Our Children**.  With a median age of 7 years. *(AFCARS)*

Imagine the huge impact a separation like this would have on <u>any</u> first grader you know, especially if they were <u>not</u> cared for in their new surroundings with an intentional investment in their long-term well-being.

And the numbers speak volumes on how The System **underinvests** in these children, committing less than 50% of what an average family spends to raise a child from birth to 17 years of age. *(iFoster)*

Without the necessary support, why would we expect young people in care to be empowered to thrive? And the story continues...

Roughly, 20,000 youth age out of the foster care system between the ages of 18 – 21 annually. Within four years of aging out, 50% will have no earnings and those who do will make an average annual income of $7,500 *(NFYI – National Foster Youth Institute)*.

There's less than a 3% chance for those who age out of foster care to earn a college degree at any point in their life. *(NFYI)*

Homelessness and unemployment become a huge issue. After reaching the age of 18, 20% of those in foster care will become instantly homeless *(NFYI)* and 29% report being homeless from age 19-21 *(Annie E. Casey Foundation - AECF).*

Just 57% of foster youth who age out of the system report being employed full- or part-time at age 21 (AECF).

Within two years of leaving care, 25% of males will be in prison, and 70% of females who age out of the foster care will become pregnant before the age of 21. *(NFYI)*

It's a tragic loss. For the children, for our society, and for our future.

**That's where we are. Let's explore how we got here.**

# Origins & Inevitable Failures of the Foster Care System

## The Orphan Train Brought Us Here.

The first orphanage in the United States was reportedly established in Mississippi in 1729, but institutional orphanages were uncommon before the early 19th century. Back then, relatives or neighbors raised children who had lost their parents. Arrangements were informal and rarely involved courts.

Around 1830, the number of American homeless children in large Eastern cities exploded. By 1850, an estimated

10,000-30,000 homeless children were among the population of 500,000 living in New York City.

Some children were orphaned when their parents died in epidemics of typhoid, yellow fever or the flu. Others were abandoned due to poverty, illness, or addiction. For protection against street violence, they banded together and formed gangs.

**This was in <u>1850</u>.**

By 1853, a New York minister became concerned with the plight of street children and founded the Children's Aid Society. Charles Loring Brace set out to offer religious, vocational, and academic instruction to children, establishing the nation's first runaway shelter to provide room, board, and basic education.

The Children's Aid Society initially attempted to find homes and jobs for individual children in New York, but they were overwhelmed by the numbers needing help, so Brace came up with a plan. His idea was to send groups of children from the East Coast to more rural areas where they could be adopted by "morally upright" farm families and raised to have better lives.

*Placements depended on what was available, children were often treated like cattle "up for adoption," siblings were separated, and there was very little oversight.*

Brace was also aware of the growing need for labor in the expanding farm country and expected farmers would welcome homeless children, take them in, and treat them as their own.

His program became known as the Department of Foster Care and the transportation of children from their home area via the railroad became known as the **"orphan train."**

Less than half the children on the trains were actual orphans and as many as 25% had two living parents. They ended up on the trains or in orphanages either because their families didn't have the means to raise them or because they had been abused and abandoned or were runaways. Sometimes older children on the train were simply in search of work or a free ticket out of the city.

Once they reached their destination, orphan train children had no choice in where they ended up. Prominent local citizens were responsible for working with the Children's Aid Society to ensure suitable placements and conditions.

Those placements depended on what was available, children were often treated like cattle "up for adoption," and siblings were separated; there was very little oversight.

The "orphans" were perceived as free labor to help with chores around the farm, with the additional expectation that families would raise them alongside their own children while providing food, clothing, shelter, education, and $100 when they turned 21.

From 1855 to 1875, the Children's Aid Society sent an average of 3,000 children on trains to 45 states each year, as well as Canada and Mexico. Orphan train children encountered ridicule and prejudice and felt like outsiders in their host families. Often, their new communities viewed them as delinquent offspring of drunks and prostitutes. Many children were forced to change their names and lost their identities in the process.

By 1929, approximately 200,000 children had traveled west by rail and were "placed" in new homes. Brace's notion was that children were better off in placements with families, rather than in institutions.

This remains a basic tenet of present-day foster care over 150 years later.

Why does this matter?

## The Orphan Train Legacy

When we begin to understand the origins of foster care, it becomes clear that the patterns of negative outcomes today are rooted in patterns, systems and mental models established a century and a half ago.

Let's follow this 19th century orphan "train of thought" - or mental model - to our 21st century system (Fig. 1).

- There are **"broken" children from "broken homes"** whose parents cannot care for them due to poverty, illness, addiction, abuse, and neglect who should be removed for the good of everyone.
- They should be **"placed" outside their communities** with new, upright foster families, if possible, and provided with basic shelter and education.
- Some children may be put **"up for adoption"** and, in the process, siblings may be separated.
- Children face **obstacles while in the system** ranging from prejudice to feeling like outsiders in family placements.
- Many people will view them **as damaged offspring of deficient addicts and lowlifes**.
- Many children can be **expected to lose their identity** through repeated moves, bouncing from one foster care placement to another, never knowing when they will be uprooted.
- Some will be further **abused in systems that are supposed to protect them**.
- Instead of being safely reunified with their families, or moved quickly into adoptive homes, many children **languish in foster care for years**.

# "Broken Children" Mental Model
Fig. 1

| | |
|---|---|
| *Broken Children, Broken Homes* | **MENTAL MODEL** What are you **THINKING** that creates the **Systems** you design? |
| *Need to be taken and Placed in Better homes* | **SYSTEMS/STRUCTURE** What are the **SYSTEMS** you putinto place that create **Behaviors** aligned with your **Thinking?** |
| *Placements Found Placements Made* | **BEHAVIOR PATTERNS** How are People **BEHAVING** based on the established **Systems** and **Thinking?** |
| *Disconnected, ill-prepared, Unsuccessful young people* | **OUTCOMES** What are the inevitable **RESULTS** of the **Thinking, Systems** and **Behaviors?** |

Brace's pre-Civil War solution for moving children off city streets persists as the prevailing "mental model" for foster care today and was the same mentality that pulled apart Native American families with devastating results, sending them to "schools" to "fix" them.

The change is the number of children impacted. According to the Children's Bureau and AFCARS Report, in FY 2021:
- At the beginning of the year, almost **400,000** children were in foster care
- An additional **207,000** children under 18 entered foster care, totaling **607,000,** and **114,000** were waiting for adoption
- Children ages 0 to 5 made up the largest share at 42%

Life Changing Choices: Just in Time for Foster Youth

Children in child welfare face profound mental health challenges and are disproportionately LGBTQ+ children of color. It's estimated that up to 80% of children in foster care suffer from a mental health issue compared to 18-22% of the general population. *(NCSL)*

Numerous studies, including a report of foster care alumni by Casey Family Programs, show that those impacted by the current foster care system have a higher prevalence of physical and psychiatric morbidity. Foster care alumni are almost twice as likely to suffer from Post-Traumatic Stress Disorder than U.S. war veterans. *(Northwest Foster Care Alumni Study)*

It's no wonder that the uncertainty, stress and persistent trauma of the foster care experience takes a staggering toll on the mental health of youth in care. (Fig 2)

**Foster Care Mental Health Disparities (NCSL)**

Fig. 2

| Mental Illness | Foster Alumni % | General Adult Pop. % |
|---|---|---|
| Post-Traumatic Stress Disorder. | 21.5 | 4.5 |
| Major Depressive Episode | 15.3 | 10.6 |
| Modified Social Phobia | 11.9 | 8.9 |
| Panic Disorder | 11.4 | 3.6 |
| Generalized Anxiety Disorder | 9.4 | 5.1 |
| Alcohol Dependence | 3.7 | 2.0 |
| Drug Dependence | 3.6 | 0.5 |
| Bulimia | 2.9 | 0.4 |

Most states lack adequate home and community-based mental health support for children and families, even though these services generally cost <u>less</u> and have better outcomes. For decades, child welfare and probation agencies in California sent foster youth and teens on probation with challenging behaviors or mental health issues to other states for care, claiming a lack of in-state options that met their complex needs. (Imprint)

When children cannot return home to their families, child welfare systems must move quickly to find them alternative placements. As time goes by and they age, the prospects for landing in safe, loving, permanent homes grow dimmer for foster youth.

Many will simply "age out" of the system when they turn 18, without a family and without the skills to make it on their own.

# Facing the Foster Care Cliff At the End of the Track

There are three additional factors that are cause for serious concern.

First, it's becoming increasingly clear that a majority of young people in foster care have endured **Adverse Childhood Experiences (ACEs)** that increase the probability of health challenges, such as dementia (4.5x), chronic pulmonary disease (2.5x) and depression (5x).

Second, the National Institute of Health finds that former foster youth are more likely than their peers from healthy families to have their own children enter the foster care system.

Finally, Black and Latinx communities are overrepresented within this system, heightening the probability that they will remain trapped in multi-generational cycles of family separation, trauma, and poverty.

The Orphan Train brought us here and, for many young people, the destination has been bleak. How can we finally find a different track to a better future?

# Intention and the Wrong Forest

If we link current outcomes to outdated and ineffective mental models that lead to the systems that fail our children, how do we create change?

One perspective can be found in Stephen Covey's 7 Habits of Highly Effective People. The story goes like this:

*A group of people are cutting their way through the forest with machetes. They're charged to be the problem solvers in the organization. They're steadfastly cutting through the undergrowth, clearing it out.*

*Their managers are behind them, sharpening their machetes, writing policy and procedure manuals, holding muscle development programs, bringing in improved cutting techniques based on the latest best practice research and setting working schedules and compensation programs for the most efficient machete wielders.*

*But somebody who is not fixed on the accepted mental model and prevailing perspective of the organization climbs the tallest tree for the clearest vision of what's happening. They survey the entire situation, and yell, "Everybody! This is the wrong forest!"*

*But the problem solvers and managers respond "Leave us alone! We're making great progress!"*

The story was offered to highlight the difference between management and leadership, but it also speaks to the way we sometimes forget to check our **INTENTION**.

Without clarity of intention, we might be unable to course correct and change our work because we don't see outside the system we're steeped in or have the vision to recognize that **different ways of thinking,** not just new ways of working, are necessary to achieve different outcomes.

Vision and courage often define leadership and, fortunately, leadership can create significant impact outside existing systems. And it can happen in a simple moment of insight. What we call a **MITTCE** (MITT-see), a *Moment In Time That Changes Everything*.

Such a MITTCE happened for a group of San Diego women who looked at the transition from foster care way back in 2003, knew that something was wrong, and decided to do something about it.

One of them was **Diane Cox**.

# These are all OUR Children: The Early Years of Just in Time

*MITTCE*
*Moment In Time That Changes Everything.*

**Diane Cox,** JIT Co-Founder & Chief Sustainability Officer

*In 2002, I was a sales representative for First American Title Insurance Company in San Diego. My primary reason for working, to support my children and put them through college debt-free, was no longer a driving force for me, and I was longing for a new purpose in my life.*

*At that time, I played in a tennis league with Jeanette Day, an attorney and advocate for foster youth in the San Diego courts. It was holiday time and Jeanette asked if I would help put together Christmas gift baskets for young people living on their own who had "emancipated" from foster care.*

*Twenty-five baskets later, Jeanette and I spent two days delivering them, and I was both inspired and horrified. Inspired by the spirit and enthusiasm of these newly-turned-18 young adults and horrified by their actual circumstances.*

*I said to myself, **"This is just wrong!"***

*I wondered how my own children would have fared without the resources, encouragement, guidance, and financial support of a loving family as they navigated college and beyond? Many of these young people had no furniture, no bed to sleep on, no dining table, no desk.*

*I shared with Jeanette that my real estate clients would know lots of people who were moving or had gently used furniture that they didn't need and, if we hired moving vans and recruited volunteers with trucks, we could transport items from those who had the stuff to those who needed it. Jeanette organized a group of friends and work associates, including JIT Co-Founder Louarn Sorkin, and Just in Time was born.*

*The Community responded with generosity and enthusiasm. Louarn was using her connections and sphere of influence to raise resources, and together we built our network of volunteers who located furnishings, held mini-drives, and donated funds. One time, we outfitted eight youth apartments from one couple that was down-sizing to a senior residence!*

*As time went on and we began to get a closer look at the realities our youth were facing, we could see that lack of furnishings was just the tip of the iceberg. One young man named Justin called in a panic because his truck had broken down, which meant he would miss college classes and lose his job. JIT immediately paid $75 to the repair shop for an alternator.*

*Many years later, Justin shared that this one seemingly small bit of help enabled him to avoid a crisis that would've derailed his life. He went on to obtain an associate degree, a bachelor's degree, and finally a Master of Science in Regulatory Affairs from Georgetown University.*

In addition to emergency and basic needs assistance, some of our participants were starting college without critical tools such as laptops, printers, school supplies and basic needs.

While their roommates had family to help them move into their dorms and cheer them on, they felt alone without anyone to believe in them or care whether they succeeded. In response, JIT Co-Founder Kathryn Vaughn launched College Bound, which rapidly became JIT's most popular service.

Another Co-Founder, Tony Hsu and his wife Jenny obtained nonprofit tax status for JIT and set up an accounting system to serve the hundreds of young people JIT was now supporting.

Over the years, JIT participants identified and created more services that would fill additional gaps faced by transition age foster youth.

Then a new Vision represented by the Seven Choices in this book came into focus when Don Wells came onboard. *-Diane*

# Why Are You Still Here?
# The "Biggest Gap"

**Don Wells,** Just in Time Chief Empowerment Officer

*I was fortunate to have been born into a stable and proud African American family, with a mother and father who met when they were still in grade school and married soon after high school. While my mother's parents gave her a model for a stable and supportive marriage, my father had to sneak away to school and faced physical punishment when his single mother discovered he had chosen to go to class rather than make money to pay the bills.*

*Somehow, despite obstacles that would probably have put him in foster care in a different time, my father managed to be the first in his family to graduate from high school.*

31

*His own unstable family life forged a fierce commitment to change the Wells narrative when he was old enough to do so.*

*Donald Wells Sr, who had an absent father, became the surrogate "father" of the neighborhood where he raised his family. He organized and coached both a boys' and girls' baseball team. Our house was a magnet for every child nearby with the only ping pong and pool table for everyone to enjoy.*

*And my mother was famous for her generosity to anyone who needed assistance. She would, literally, give away her last dollar to someone with an urgent need.*

*I believe that every family has an invisible word or phrase engraved over their front door. For the Wells family, those words would have been Responsibility and Abundance. I took those words with me as I tried to find my place in the world.*

*"Why are you still here?"*

*I took a step closer to that goal while working at a local TV station in San Diego. The shock of the Columbine school shootings in April 1999 inspired me to use my position overseeing Community Affairs to recruit male mentors for young men who might otherwise take the same destructive path. The campaign goal was to sign up 1,000 men by Father's Day. I was one of those thousand.*

*I became a mentor to Victor, a bright nine-year-old, and his younger sister by one year, Belen. They had already been in and out of the foster care system for many years before we met and, a few months into our connection, they found themselves back in care with Jeanette Day as their lawyer advocate, three years before Just in Time was born.*

*I also began to see what was in store for them. On one day, when Belen was 11 years old, we'd been watching a movie together when she suddenly turned to me and asked,*
   ***"Why are you still here?"***

*At that moment, our three-year connection was her longest, continuous relationship ever with a caring adult. That's when it fully hit me: No young person should ever have to ask themselves why truly caring and committed adults are still in their lives.*

*So, I said yes when Jeanette asked me to come to the launch of a new nonprofit. I was there on the first planning day for Just in Time for Foster Youth in 2003 and served as a volunteer over the next six years as I continued to remain a constant in the lives of Victor and Belen.*

*I joined the JIT Board in 2009 and within a few months was asked to become the Executive Director for an organization with a powerful mission, one staff member, and the enormous potential to create change.*

*For me, the first element of change was to take the lesson I learned from Belen, the importance of lasting Connection, and apply it to Just in Time's core belief about young people impacted by foster care. -**Don***

# Building Reliable, Responsive, Real Community

Before 2010, JIT's volunteer-staffed organization had consistently expanded programs to meet the growing needs of youth leaving foster care, reaching an annual budget of $84,000 in 2006 when it was granted 501(c)3 status and funding of nearly $400,000 by 2009.

The stated mission was *"to provide emancipated foster youth with **opportunities for self-sufficiency** through emergency support, essential resources, **and caring personal guidance** at critical junctures on their path to independence."*

The goal was to assist San Diego's transition age foster youth 18-26 with attaining and sustaining self-sufficiency levels significantly higher than the national average.

*The key to real transformation in transition was within our reach.*

That meant: significantly improving their chances of securing steady employment with decent pay and benefits; establishing and sustaining stable housing; responsibly managing their finances for the long term; forming families that they can support; steering clear of the criminal justice system; and making meaningful contributions throughout the San Diego community.

Initially, meeting that goal in the short-term made us feel good about being helpful.

But it became clear that filling gaps in resources wasn't enough.

As young people continued to exit the child welfare system unprepared for adulthood, and with their transition uncertain, fragmented and difficult, we were fortunate that the key to real transformation in transition was within our reach. The one critical thing no one had found a way to provide consistently was actually an enormous untapped resource we could access – **reliable relationships** within a caring community of volunteers.

That's when, in 2010, Just in Time's mission changed focus.

## Paradigms, Purpose and People

While "opportunities for self-sufficiency" with "caring personal guidance" was clearly a good intention, our new commitment created a larger promise to the youth we served.

**"To engage a caring community** to help transition age foster youth achieve self-sufficiency **and well-being"** was established as the primary starting point for everything JIT offered.

While there were obvious gaps to be filled in access to housing, transportation, education and employment, we realized that the **most important gap that foster youth face is a lifetime of disconnection** – first from family, then being moved from place to place within a system, and finally being pushed into the world without the reliable, lasting relationships that all young people need.

*Our Words create our Reality.*

The fierce commitment to end the disconnection for young people like Belen, who had no expectation of lasting relationships, became the reason Just in Time exists.

That means the lingering assumptions from the Orphan Train era had to be challenged and set aside.

And the words used to describe foster youth, their families, and their potential needed a long overdue examination because our words create our reality and precede our actions.

## That's the power of a shift in Mental Models that leads to <u>real</u> change.

Different assumptions and beliefs change expectations and encourage innovation, unleashing the power of everyone in our community.

A clear set of principles and practices began to take shape that has driven our work ever since. (Fig. 3)

Fig. 3

| Just in Time for Foster Youth Mental Model |
| --- |
| **Principle 1:** A life of Uncertainty and Disconnection is the core obstacle for transition age foster youth, therefore **Consistent Connection** is the core solution.<br>**Practice:** We engage youth in consistent relationships with volunteers whenever possible. |
| **Principle 2:** We employ **Staff with Lived Experience** because there is tremendous power in seeing yourself in the person you reach out to when you must Share your Story and be vulnerable. And more power in being able to see your possible success in theirs. **Practice:** We employ former foster youth as staff in service delivery and other leadership roles. |
| **Principle 3:** Without **Real Trust**, there can be no lasting transformative connection.<br>**Practice:** We stress authentic relationships in all  contacts. |
| **Principle 4:** Every youth is **Unique**.<br>**Practice:** We stress individualized approaches to all services, with participants as our collaborative partners. |
| **Principle 5:** Every youth has the power to create their **Own Success**. Well-being is only possible with a **Wholistic Understanding** of what is truly needed.<br>**Practice:** We focus on all aspects of youth needs, not only the presenting issue. |
| **Principle 6:** **Timely Intervention** at a critical juncture is the difference between hope and despair.<br>**Practice:** We respond proactively to needs as they arise, both for the individual and the population as a whole. |
| **Principle 7:** Meeting the dynamically changing needs of youth requires **Curiosity, Creativity and Courage**.<br>**Practice:** We constantly evolve our services by keeping our "finger on the pulse" of youth need. |

With this foundation, it was necessary to discard the "Broken Children" mental model and replace it with a new way of thinking (below) that leads to very different outcomes (Fig. 4)

- Our participants are **Creative, Resourceful and Whole** who grew up in challenging environments, not "broken" children from "broken homes"

- Our participants are invited to **connect to our community**, not "placed" in programs that only meet their most basic needs

- Our participants join our community voluntarily as we help them **meet their own identified goals** as partners in their success

- Our participants won't feel the need to distance themselves from the foster care experience but will come to **embrace their identity** as part of a powerful, resilient community

- Our participants will **see themselves as role models, inspiring and exceptional** people with bright futures

- Our participants will take **ownership of their story and identity**, with a strong internal sense of self and personal power

- Our participants will **create our community** as Coordinators, Managers, Directors and Volunteers to keep us honest and effective

- Our participants will not only "learn how to fish" but will **join a "fishing village"** that they can rely on for a sense of belonging and support

# Creative, Resourceful & Whole
## Mental Model

Fig. 4

| | |
|---|---|
| *Connected, Confident Successful young people* | **OUTCOMES** What are the inevitable RESULTS **of the** Thinking, Systems **and Behaviors?** |
| *Connections Made* | **BEHAVIOR PATTERNS** How are People **BEHAVING** based on the established **Systems** and **Thinking?** |
| *Need to be Partners in a Reliable Community* | **SYSTEMS/STRUCTURE** What are **SYSTEMS** you put into place that create **Behaviors** aligned with your **Thinking?** |
| *Youth are Creative, Resourceful & Whole* | **MENTAL MODEL** What are you **THINKING** that creates the **Systems** you design? |

Building a caring community of volunteers and peers for thousands of young people, now close to 3,000 youth in San Diego annually, is what Just in Time has done for almost two decades. Community begins from the moment a youth comes in and they're greeted by our lived experience staff. That first encounter immediately builds a sense of trust because they've both been there. Unstable, uncertain, but full of hope.

The community approach, driven by the youth we served and based on measurable impact and benefit, was what propelled the growth of services and resources, and expanded that $400,000 budget in 2009 to $6,000,000 in 2022, *without state or federal funding*.

# Life Changing Choices

Rather than continuing to "temporarily" outsource the welfare of our children to systems that have failed them, this shift to a new mental model requires us to build a foundation of lasting positive relationships. It replicates how any healthy family creates a successful transition for its children from birth to adulthood.

The social service narrative of "**Programs/Systems**" is replaced by a people-centered, volunteer-driven **"Services /Community**" framework for delivery of comprehensive resources and access to reliable relationships.

We also recognize the young people we serve as **Creative, Resourceful, and Whole** - not damaged and deficient — so we partner with them as leaders in the development of our community. Former foster youth staff and participants are integral to every JIT event, presentation, and communication, acting as Lead voices at all significant gatherings.

In fact, **more than half of our current staff are former foster youth**, most of them having participated in JIT services. Our youth-centered approach creates a real community of young people who volunteer for JIT, become peer coaches to the youth who follow, and take ownership of the organization. JIT doesn't just serve youth; it embodies and celebrates their promise and power to shape their futures.

**Just in Time is uniquely focused on creating a lasting community of support for young people impacted by foster care so they can thrive and become Confident, Capable and Connected.**

For any organization seeking durable, transformative change, there are choices to be made – significant, life-altering choices. After twenty years, we've identified the keys factors that have been vital to our success.

The next seven chapters describe the 7 Essential Choices we faced and made, which we believe were the key to our lasting and transformative impacts.

Rather than a "How to" guide, what comes next is more of a "Why do" story about the decisions we make to serve **OUR** children.

# The 7 Essential Choices

**Choice 1:** What's Your Intention? *(Prioritize Protection or Empowerment)*

**Choice 2**: Who are You Serving? *(See Damaged & Broken or Creative, Resourceful & Whole)*

**Choice 3:** What will You Promise? *(Build a System or a Community)*

**Choice 4:** Where will You Find Answers? *(Act from YOUR Agenda or Listen to Lived Experience Experts)*

**Choice 5:** When will You Know You're Succeeding? *(Report What was Done or Share What had Lasting Impact)*

**Choice 6:** How will You Sustain Your Efforts? *(Follow the Funding or Engage with Impact)*

**Choice 7:** Who can Start THIS Where You Live? *(Wait for Someone Else or Be the Needed Change)*

Together, we **can** get off the Orphan "Train of Thought" if we make the new Choices to better serve the young people who depend on us to consistently care about what is truly in their best interest.

## We can do better….and we <u>must</u>.

## PART 1 Takeaways

- The American child welfare system is built on assumptions from the **1850's** - underlying beliefs, thinking and logic that have led to unacceptable outcomes today.

- The long-held belief is that **"broken" children** from "broken homes" should be "placed" outside their communities and "up for adoption."

- These children are often viewed as incorrigible offspring of addicts and lowlifes and some will be **further abused in systems that are supposed to protect them.**

- Old mental models have led to systems, policies and procedures that encourage aligned behaviors which produce current **unhealthy results.**

- Instead of being safely reunified with their families — or moved quickly into adoptive homes — **many children will languish in foster care for years.**

- Suffering from **disconnection** and a lack of foundational life skills and resources, young people exit the system with dire consequences for themselves and the larger community.

- For any organization seeking to create durable, transformative change, there are **choices to be made** — significant, life-altering choices. The next seven chapters will describe the 7 Essential Choices we faced and made, which we believe were the key to our highly successful impacts.

**Join the Life Changing Movement at**
**jitfosteryouth.org/100KCommunity**

JIT Participants in
Reliable, Responsive, Real Community

# Part 2

# The 7 Essential Choices

## *"New Memories in a World of My Own Making"*
## Zane's Story

*On the day I was born, my mother was diagnosed with an illness and I remember that, two days before my sixth birthday, my wonderful mother died. My dad returned from the military but, rather than a happy reunion like you'd find on Instagram, I remember a monster who was so angry he took it out on me. He held so much hate in his heart, there was one thing I knew to be true: I never wanted to be anything like him. On top of that, food was scarce, and the question "Will I eat today?" created such instability that it still haunts my eating habits to this day.*

*Little did I know that abuse and neglect were not love. Little did I know that a father was capable of hating someone whom he was meant to love. Little did I know that this is the weight I will carry for the rest of my life. It wasn't until I became violently ill that I realized the danger I was in. I remember experiencing neurocardiogenic episodes in which I'd lose my vision, hearing, balance and, finally, my consciousness. These episodes would occur upwards of 20 times a day and they were extremely painful both physically and mentally.*

*There are so many memories I could recount. The time my dad tried to shoot me. Or the time my brother tried to light me on fire. Memories of growing up way too fast because I had no other choice. After spending years on this treacherous path, I remember I had to make a choice: stay and suffer a harsh fate or leave and build a future for myself. So, I ran away at age 15, striving for the new life that I am still building today. Despite the challenges of my past, I managed to graduate high school and ranked 7 out of 400 students.*

*In 2019, I found Just in Time, or rather JIT found me, thanks to JIT alum and staff member, Simone. She recruited me to join her Rise to Resilience service, and that was the first time I met other students with backgrounds similar to mine. This was when I knew I wasn't alone anymore.*

*Soon after, JIT helped me with the purchase of new tires. Little did I know that driving around on fifteen-year-old tires was dangerous. Needless to say, I got those new tires just in time! And one of the most practical benefits of JIT has been Financial Fitness, where I'm learning how to plan for my future, including saving, investments and retirement.*

*Now I'm a student at a four-year university, pursuing a bachelor's in Music as well as General Theatre Studies with a minor in social and personality psychology. I aspire to earn a master's and become a professor and a thespian.*

*Hearing my story, you might think I've gone through a lot, even though I'm only 20 years old, and you'd be right. It might surprise you to know that, as I look back on my life, I wouldn't change a thing because every choice, every adverse experience and bad memory has led me to where I am today...with a future of new friends and new opportunities.*

*Just in Time, college, theatre.... these are all **NEW** memories.... in a world of **MY** own making. And I look forward to a lifetime of new memories ahead of me. – **Zane***

**Empowered Student & Volunteer Coach**
*JIT College Bound*

# Choice One
## *What's Your Intention?*

### Prioritize Protection or Empowerment

Alice: Would you tell me, please, which way I ought to go from here?

Cheshire Cat: That depends a good deal on where you want to get to.

Alice: I don't much care where.

Cheshire Cat: Then it doesn't much matter which way you go.
Lewis Carroll
From Alice in Wonderland

# A Lesson from the Cheshire Cat

How do we get <u>off</u> the Orphan Train after all this time?

We can find a clue in a 2009 talk to fifty people in a small room given by Simon Sinek, which has become one of the most-watched talks on TED.com.

Sinek's message was about the power of starting every effort with your **WHY**. Your purpose, cause or belief. WHY do you get out of bed every morning? WHY does your organization exist?

And WHY should anyone care?

If your WHY is fuzzy, it's more difficult to achieve any sort of success, inspire others or maintain an effort when things become challenging.

Knowing your WHY means having an **Intention** that is crystal clear. Otherwise, we might end up like Alice. Wandering down a road with low expectations or unsatisfactory outcomes.

If your WHY actually has you heading toward negative results, efficiently cutting your way through the wrong forest, you might wonder what went awry.

A clear sense of WHY sets expectations. When we don't know our WHY, we don't know what to expect, so we accept whatever happens.

To effectively exit the legacy of the Orphan Train means more than deciding where we want to go next.

It's deciding WHY we're doing what we do in the first place.

**That's the First Choice we make**.

# The Choice to Protect

When Charles Loring Brace founded the Children's Aid Society in 1853, his goal was protection.

With tens of thousands of homeless children roaming the streets of major cities, one of the primary motivations was to protect the citizens of those cities from the "broken" youth who were threatening their sense of safety and order.

*In some cases, Protection is imposed...so those who are being "protected" have no voice.* And he also sought to protect the children from moral and economic risk by offering them to be "placed" and raised by those who could offer them work and the possibility of a good life through the Department of Foster Care, the ancestor of Child "Protective" Services.

**The Choice to Protect can be essential** as an urgent matter and a first step. The vulnerable may need protection from harm, abuse and exploitation.

To Protect is to make sure someone is not injured or mistreated. It may be necessary at times, but **not the end goal**.

In some cases, Protection is imposed, not offered, so those who are being "protected" have no voice, even if they are in the position to express their own preferences.

When Protection becomes the central WHY, the <u>only</u> identified Intention, it can constrain and diminish those who are "protected" by avoiding "risky" choices and minimizing growth experiences with limiting, risk-averse policies, procedures, and systems.

# The Choice to Empower

In contrast, the Choice to Empower embraces the idea that human growth requires trial and error, failures and successes, and the authority to make the decisions that lead to our eventual self-confidence and competence. (Fig 5) Mistakes are inevitable. In fact, mistakes are a critical part of the learning process!

*True Empowerment is different from the top-down version where an individual is pressured to accept more responsibilities without being provided the requisite training and tools.*

Fig. 5

| Child *Protective* Services | Child *Empowerment* Services |
|---|---|
| Judge the parents of children in struggling families | Work with families as partners to understand their needs |
| Remove children from struggling families until they are "fixed" | Work with families to understand their needs and provide resources |
| Place children where they will be safe for the short term | Create connections for children to strengthen them for the long term |
| Create a culture of hiding and shame and fearful uncertainty | Create a culture of possibility and pride for the children served |
| Success measured in avoiding terrible headlines | Success measured in positive impacts and thriving adults |

To Empower, it's critical to understand the person's character and experience, strengths and weaknesses, motivations, and aspirations.

The responsibility and accountability lie with the person who is being empowered.

But this doesn't mean leaving the individual entirely on their own. A delicate balance is needed and achieved by open discussion and continuous inquiry around the topics of vision, priorities, future challenges, and what more is needed to succeed.

True Empowerment is different from the top-down version where an individual is pressured to accept more responsibilities without being provided the requisite training and tools. Worse, those who practice top-down "empowerment" blame those who "fail" them when the desired outcome is not achieved!

## A Mental Model & Theory of Change Grounded in Empowerment

In the 1990's, a new way of analyzing programs and initiatives working to promote social change emerged. A "Theory of Change" defines long-term goals and then maps backward to identify necessary conditions to ensure the goals are met.

By 2012, Just in Time had established its Theory of Change and Measurable Success, along with the principles behind each feature. Our objective was and is to build a long "bridge" of Empowerment for youth after 18 until 27 as young people transition from care with consistent youth-centered support tied to specific intended impacts.

JIT's Theory of Change suggests that if we assist young people impacted by foster care to become Confident, Capable and Connected, they will also become self-sufficient with a sense of well-being and life satisfaction for the long-term, breaking the cycle of foster care.

Our Theory of Change emerged from the Mental Model mentioned previously, which included seven principles and accompanying practices (Fig 3, page 36). Throughout the years, it has remained constant as our foundational platform on which JIT services have been built. And empowered youth have provided us with the feedback we need to evolve and succeed.

In fact, it was our JIT participants who identified the four key drivers of durable transformation:

1. **Exposure to knowledge and experiences** that lead to a more expanded and expressive view of life, which increases their credibility and ability to solve the problems at hand.
2. **Learning self-awareness, including their strengths, self-limiting beliefs, and value,** plus understanding their place in the world once they then realize they are no different than "successful" people.
3. **Gaining the power of owning and sharing their own stories** and converting a painful past into a source of empathy, proactivity and confidence.
4. **Establishing authentic, mutually supportive relationships** that foster healthy personal and professional boundaries and result in lasting connections based on consistency and trust.

Subsequent research has shown that these four outcomes create a mutually reinforcing "tipping point" for deep, durable change in self-perception and personal empowerment.

Using the Mental Model and Four Drivers of Transformational Change as our guide, JIT has developed innovative, individualized empowering services that meet the expressed needs of our youth. And, because chances of achieving self-sufficiency increase exponentially when youth have relationships with one or more caring adults, life-affirming relationships are at the heart of all the work we do and incorporated into all our services.

**2003  My First Home** Transforms empty apartments into safe, stable and supportive places to live with new and gently used furnishings from our caring community

**2004  Basic Needs** Lends essential support to overcome life's inevitable emergency situations, including rent assistance, bus passes, gas cards, grocery cards, clothing and vehicle repairs, always with the intention to connect to a caring community

**2006  College Bound/Learning to Succeed** Provides the critical resources, tools, connections, and encouragement every scholar needs to attain their academic dreams, including internships and study abroad

**2010  Financial Fitness** Develops healthy money management habits for lifelong financial stability, from foundational budgeting and saving skills to long term investment strategies

**2011  Career Horizons for Young Women** Exposes young women to a broad variety of professional paths while they build a strong sense of self and make meaningful connections to female coaches

**2014  JIT Coach Approach** embeds principles and practices in our culture based on the belief that we are all creative, resourceful and whole with the capacity to access our inner wisdom to create the lives we want and build community.

**2015 Changing Lanes/Auto Access** Fills a critical transportation gap with driver training, obtaining licenses, and purchasing reliable vehicles and insurance at affordable rates

**2015 Pathways to Financial Power** Provides career readiness skills, explores a wide range of employment opportunities to match one's strengths, offers job opportunities, and supports entrepreneurial ventures

**2016 Master Your Dream** Offers financial scholarships for students enrolled in Graduate School or Law School – 100% of all Master Your Dream scholars have successfully attained their degrees

**2019 NEXTjobs** "NEXT" stands for New (readiness for first/better jobs); Entrepreneurship (building capacity for self-employment); X/Unknown (training for the jobs of the future); Trades (access to well-paying jobs like electrical, construction, etc.), with individualized training, contacts, financial resources, ongoing support

**2019 Rise to Resilience/Mental Wellness** Educates about the negative impacts of Adverse Childhood Experiences (ACES) and how to build resilience with the benefit of Community and seven healthy practices, including access to healing-centered therapy

**2020 Housing from the Heart** Provides housing stipends for undergraduate and graduate college students to reduce financial pressures and allow a focus on academic success

## The intention to Empower is the First Choice.

## How we See Those Being Served is next.

# Choice One Essential Takeaways

- When the **Choice to Protect** is pursued as the central WHY, the <u>only</u> identified Intention, it can constrain and diminish those who are "protected" by avoiding "risky" choices and minimizing growth experiences with limiting, risk-averse policies, procedures, and systems.

- **The Choice to Empower** embraces the idea that human growth requires trial and error, failures and successes, and the authority to make the decisions that lead to our eventual self-confidence and competence.

- **Responsibility and accountability lie with the person being empowered**, who also must be understood and armed with the tools to succeed.

- A **Theory of Change and Mental Model grounded in Empowerment** can serve as the foundational platform for one's services.

- Those served are **empowered to succeed and guide** the improvement and evolution of the services.

**Join the Life Changing Movement at jitfosteryouth.org/100KCommunity**

**Resourceful JIT Participant & Coach**
*Pathways to Financial Power*

# Choice Two
## *Who Are You Serving?*

## See Damaged & Broken or Creative, Resourceful, & Whole

*Damaged or broken sends the message that we're beyond repair –
a lost cause. The lens of creative, resourceful, and whole empowers
us to find our true selves which we were taught not to see.*
                    *Irving Chavez*
                    *Chief Impact Officer, Just in Time*

# The Choice to See Damaged & Broken

When first encountering a person who experienced the foster care system, it's far too common to focus on the "misfortune" that they experienced to get them there.  As with the Choice to Protect, this perspective may initially be based in compassion but often produces disempowering justifications to treat youth as incapable and unable to make decisions on their own behalf - the perspective of broken home, broken family and, ultimately, the "broken person" we spoke of earlier.

It elicits pity, oversimplifies the experiences of the person with the lived experience, and creates an expectation of trying to fix and repair. This also reinforces the young person's perception of themselves as helpless and a burden: "I have no ability or power to overcome anything that comes my way."

This negative narrative is seen through a lens that identifies youth as the central problem (what's wrong with them/me) and solutions that stem from that view (involuntary therapy, punitive "fixes," etc.) For the lived experience youth, that view becomes internalized as self-limiting saboteurs (what's wrong with me) that whisper and shout:

*"Terrible things always happen to me. If I make a mistake, everyone is going to jump down my throat. I'm flawed. I wish someone would help me. I want to trust people, but I'm suspicious of their motives. This is just too much. Maybe if I let it go, it will take care of itself. If I get into conflict with others, I might lose my connection with them."*

**If we see someone as Damaged and Broken, it puts the focus on our role as Rescuer, Fixer, and Savior,** which may feed our need for significance and being the hero, but it does not support Empowerment no matter how good our intentions might be.

**Irving Chavez**, JIT's Chief Impact Officer, experienced that lack of empowerment.

## Becoming the Adult Me My Child Self would have Felt Safe With

*As I entered Foster Care just shy of the tender age of 2 years old, I was "too young" to remember the reasons behind the separations from my biological parents and sometimes even my siblings. The only consistency I experienced was the lack of it.*

*Throughout my formative years and multiple placements, moving from state to state, country to country, I always felt different. Decisions were being made for me, as expected for a child, but by adults who were inadequate and unable to cope, thus creating a mindset of constant caution and hypervigilance.*

*This hypervigilance gradually became my biggest weakness. I felt like I was put together by the Powers That Be but in the wrong order. I felt estranged from reality as if life was happening to me, not by choice or by will, but just happening.  This caused me to feel powerless, directionless, and not capable.*

*After years of emotional and physical instability, my life took a turn when one of my older sisters took guardianship of me.*

*This is where MY life began.*

*I entered the educational system for the first time in high school. I didn't know I'd need a bathroom pass, or what a "school bell" signified, or how to tackle subjects like English, algebra, and history. Suddenly, I had to deal with the complicated dynamics of teenage life as well as a barrage of unfamiliar systems, norms, authorities, and societal expectations.*

*I made many age-appropriate mistakes – dating the wrong people, not setting boundaries in friendships, and over-criticizing myself. In my overly cautious and self-critical mind, it was all catastrophic. I truly believed I could never become anything because I was broken, misassembled, and lost. How could I expect anything else?*

*It was not until my final year at high school when my older brothers encouraged me to pursue higher education that I began to see how I might be able to impact my own life in a big way. Before then, this concept had been completely foreign to me. I perceived my 3.8 GPA, 250+ hours of community service, and a medal for completing the only women's studies class in California as the endpoint of my success. All I was striving to do was make it to the next day and the next one after that.*

*The reasons I grew up believing I was "broken" were actually my greatest strengths.*

*But higher education was a totally different experience. College wasn't about the subject or the degree for me, but about my own growth... to better understand myself and to expose myself to things I'd never had the opportunity to explore. Realizing I'd been living in the wake of other people's mistakes my entire life, with no explanation of how that came about, I pursued a bachelor's in Chemistry with a Biochemistry emphasis in order to make more sense of the world and my place in it.*

*After graduating, I applied for a full-time position at Just in Time. I had been a JIT participant and, by the time I applied, I knew that the characteristics I had previously seen as proof that I was "broken" were, in reality, my greatest strengths. The hypervigilance had morphed into social awareness and, ultimately, self-awareness. It enabled me to meet my needs and the needs of others without believing it was my responsibility to change why they felt the way they did.*

*I felt less broken. I stopped seeking explanations for the mysteries surrounding my upbringing and began to grasp that the ways I interpreted and responded to my environment as a child were understandable and appropriate. And with that insight, I can now say that I am becoming the adult me that my child self would have felt safe with.* **- Irving**

**Empowering someone you see as Broken** is attempting to light a fire using fuel that is damp and resistant to flame. Too often, we invite and encourage dependence which makes it difficult to support the Choice to Empower.

## That's the Second Choice we make.

# The Choice to See Creative, Resourceful, and Whole

When we shift our perspective to view ourselves and others as creative, resourceful, and whole, the unproductive narrative changes to an empowering: "I can develop and learn from my experience to overcome what happened to me."

The power dynamic shifts.

r is no longer in the hands of an outsider who may come, causing us to latch on to the painful void of what we are missing. Instead, there is acceptance of what happened and the recognition that the ability, knowledge, and strength exist within us to create what we want to happen. Our mind and our world expand from a locked and endless tunnel vision to a robust landscape of possibilities.

*The identity Marker of Former Foster Youth is a heavy and loud one.*

The Choice to see youth as Creative, Resourceful, and Whole is to respect their power and wisdom, to recognize their inner knowledge and their capacity to make their own life changing choices.

So why isn't this choice made more often?

It's an easy concept to grasp but it takes practice and time to use it effectively. In part, it's because we're not taught to think this way. Also, we have a tendency to view another person's "misfortune" through the lens and experience of our own good fortune.

This Second Choice is also powerful because it is grounded in identity. The identity marker of "former foster youth" is a heavy and loud one, sometimes superseding cultural, age, ethnic, gender identity, sexuality, geographic and all other markers.

For those who have experienced care, especially at an early age, think of all the courtroom visits, Child Protective Services (CPS) check-ins, police encounters, permission slips, and paperwork to be filled out where you're grilled for family information. Children find themselves mired in a system that was not created by them but ends up being a shared experience of dissatisfaction, disconnection, shame, and secrecy.

How can these children not have a sense of collective negative identity?

When communicating and experiencing another person as Whole, rather than deficient, the person with lived experience also begins to see themselves the same way, gaining a greater sense of control and decision-making. The job they want does not seem as unattainable, the relationship they can't seem to break off no longer seems as critical to keep just because of the fear of being alone.

Resourcefulness increases as the idea that we are capable starts to take hold and the ways we believe in ourselves begin to strengthen. We learn we can create solutions and believe we can have and deserve the relationships that support our goals.

Finally, creativity gives us the power to source out alternatives when our current solutions don't provide the outcomes we need/desire, which increases our confidence that we do have the capacity to attain our desired goals.

These are the underlying dynamics of Just in Time's Coach Approach and Rise to Resilience, both expressions of the Choice to see youth as Creative, Resourceful, and Whole.

---

**Creative** with the potential to dream big and design a life of your own choosing

**Resourceful** with the skills, resources, and talents to move from surviving to thriving

**Whole** where traumatic experiences can be re-framed from broken or damaged to resilient and abundant

---

# The Just in Time Coach Approach:
## Communication that Builds Community & Deepens Connection

The bedrock of JIT's Coach Approach is the foundational premise that every human being is Creative, Resourceful, and Whole, capable of discovering one's own Truth and Life Path. The Intention of the JIT Coach Approach is to help us access our inner wisdom.

The ways we gain this access are by practicing presence, active listening, inquiry, and affirmation - simple communication methods that deepen connections with one another and help to untangle difficult emotions and thoughts, thus illuminating our paths and our options.

Originally designed to be a tool for teaching effective mentorship, the JIT Coach Approach has now expanded to include three additional pillars: Relationships, Healing, and Networking.

The foundational Principles of the JIT Coach Approach are:

**Presence**
*We give our full, undivided attention, resisting our tendency to react or advise*

**Agreement/Affirmation**
*We start conversations with a positive statement that expresses what we can agree on, and we end conversations with words of appreciation for what has been shared*

**Curiosity**
*We ask questions to fill in gaps in information, discovering details we might need to know to fully understand the situation*

66

### Understanding
*We seek first to understand and clarify, rather than make assumptions*

### Acceptance
*We make a conscious choice to let go of our opinions, beliefs, and desires to meet another individual where they are right now, without judgment*

### Empowerment
*We ask powerful questions that speak to underlying issues, expand thinking, and promote insight*

The JIT Coach Approach trainings are highly interactive. Working in triads, each person takes turns in the role of coach, coach partner, and observer. A trained Coach Facilitator Observer (CFO) guides the conversations to ensure that the individual practicing the role of coach is effectively building proficiency in these core Practices:

**Active Listening -** Where we repeat or restate what the coach partner is sharing to confirm and clarify what is being shared. Active Listening enables us to make sure we hear what the other person intends to convey and any emotions they are experiencing. It requires us to be truly present and is the highest form of listening because it builds rapport and trust.  At its core, Active Listening is about understanding rather than judging.

**Curious Questions** - Where we ask questions that fill gaps in information and elicit details that might increase our understanding. We resist our tendency to share our own experiences and opinions or to give advice. In this way, curious questions empower us to replace "telling" with "asking," giving both the coach partner and coach the opportunity to gain greater clarity about the situation/issue being addressed.

**Powerful Questions** - Where we ask questions that foster a larger perspective, such as "What are you learning?" or "What is your ideal outcome?" or "What would you do if you couldn't fail?" Powerful questions replace our tendency to "fix" someone's problems with the intention to "empower" them to discover their own solutions.

**Setting Aside Our Agenda** (Fig.6) – A critical element of effective communication when practicing the JIT Coach Approach is setting aside our <u>agenda</u>. The first step is to recognize we have one, which is simply everything we know, believe, and feel - the lens through which we see the world. Then, we make a conscious decision to set aside our agenda that prompts us to **judge, tell and fix**. Instead, we make a different choice: to **understand, ask, and empower**.

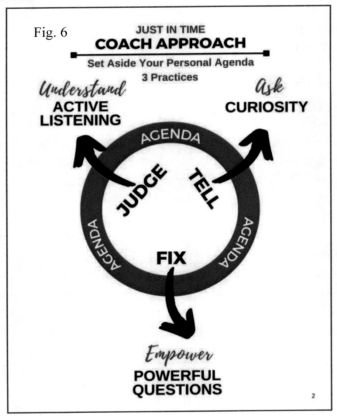

Fig. 6

JUST IN TIME
**COACH APPROACH**
Set Aside Your Personal Agenda
3 Practices

*Understand*
**ACTIVE LISTENING**

*Ask*
**CURIOSITY**

AGENDA
JUDGE
TELL
AGENDA
AGENDA
FIX

*Empower*
**POWERFUL QUESTIONS**

## What Participants say about JIT Coach Approach

*"Listening is an expression of love and giving. I was surprised how easy it was for me to talk when I just had someone listening." - **Zane***

*"I realized that, when my friends talk to me, I'm not really listening because I'm just trying to fix every little thing, and it's good to learn that it's not my job to fix – it's my job to listen and I'm learning how to do that." - **Irene***

*"It's really comforting to hear someone repeat back to me what they've heard. It makes me feel really heard - it's like an affirmation." – **Angie***

## What Volunteers say about JIT Coach Approach

*"The JIT Coach Approach helped me realize that it's not about me, even if I can relate to the situation being presented. It's about learning to really listen and understand the other person."- **Ana***

*"I've been taught through the years that my response to your talking is to say what I want to say, rather than simply listening to what you want me to hear. That takes years of un-training." - **David***

*"If I can stay present and outside of my own agenda, even if there isn't an obvious solution in the moment, I may not realize what gift I'm giving now, tomorrow, or even two weeks from now. Just because I stayed present and truly listened." - **Sally***

# The Impact of ACEs

Seeing ourselves and one another as creative, resourceful, and whole, rather than broken and deficient, also led us to an entirely new way of viewing childhood trauma, which Irving described so poignantly in the story about his growing up. A Kaiser Healthcare physician, Dr. Vincent J. Felitti, and Healthcare Clinic pioneer Dr. Nadine Burke-Harris have produced groundbreaking research on **Adverse Childhood Experiences (ACEs).**

---

### Adverse Childhood Experiences (ACEs) Survey

Prior to your 18th birthday, did you:

1. Feel that you didn't have enough to eat, had to wear dirty clothes, or had no one to protect or take care of you?
2. Lose a parent through divorce, abandonment, death, or other reason?
3. Live with anyone who was depressed, mentally ill, or attempted suicide?
4. Live with anyone who had a problem with drinking or using drugs, including prescription drugs?
5. Have parents or adults in your home who ever hit, punch, beat, or threatened to harm each other?
6. Live with anyone who went to jail or prison?
7. Have a parent or adult in your home who would ever swear at you, insult you, or put you down?
8. Have a parent or adult in your home who ever hit, beat, kick, or physically hurt you in any way?
9. Feel that no one in your family loved you or thought you were special?
10. Experience unwanted sexual contact?

Your ACE score is the total number of checked responses.

---

**Vanessa Davis**, a long-time leader within the JIT community as a participant, staff member and consultant, shares her own journey to empowerment, from her awareness of ACEs to the evolution of **Rise to Resilience**.

## Just in Time's Rise to Resilience

*As a JIT participant and staff member, the aspect of JIT that has always resonated with me is the way JIT sees its participants - not as marginalized, disadvantaged, or needing to be fixed, but as Creative, Resourceful, and Whole.*

*As a young woman who has experienced immense trauma throughout my life, the belief that JIT had in me when I first came to the organization had a profound impact. I felt I was seen and viewed as a whole person, and I committed to helping other young people feel the same.*

*When I joined the JIT staff in 2014 as a service coordinator, I genuinely believed I was at a new stage in my life, having achieved self-sufficiency and stability, well on my way to success. I quickly learned, however, that the issues of my past would not simply resolve themselves. In fact, they aggressively made themselves known, causing disruption in my life.*

*While the JIT community saw me as a strong and capable role model, I did not see myself this way. I was deeply insecure, battling imposter syndrome, anxiety, and insomnia, as well as struggling with addictive, high-risk behaviors.*

*As I battled these struggles silently and in shame, I continued to grow as a professional at JIT; it's like the organization just wouldn't stop believing in me!*

*When I moved into a management role, I noticed the same subtle fears, doubts, and anxieties in my co-workers who also identified as former foster youth. In the interactions I had with participants, I recognized the feelings of inadequacy and despair they expressed as I, too, carried that all too familiar weight. In retrospect, I realize we were all just trying our best to be okay. Yet many of us were silently suffering with the unhealed traumas of our past.*

*In 2018, JIT co-founder Diane Cox gave me a book titled, "The Deepest Well," by Dr. Nadine Burke Harris. Dr. Harris is a pediatrician who became the first Surgeon General of California. In her book, she explored how early childhood experiences impact the developing brain and body of a child and she addressed the effects of those experiences into adulthood. Diane was adamant that I read the book and, as I did, my shame and silence were challenged.*

*Adverse Childhood Experiences, or ACEs, are traumatic experiences over which a child has no control. These experiences can have lifelong implications for the child's health and future success.*

*When I learned about ACEs, it was the first time I realized the gravity of the trauma I had experienced in my childhood and the correlation between those experiences and the way I was living my life. I slowly stopped feeling ashamed of how I was living and started researching how I could heal. Thus, my personal healing journey began.... a journey that changed the way I see myself and how I see others whose lives are burdened by early trauma.*

*When left unaddressed, ACEs lead to an increase in an array of negative health consequences, including obesity, heart disease, anxiety, depression, emphysema, cancer, unintended pregnancies, suicide, and even premature death. Research by the Administration for Children and Families revealed that a score of at least 4 ACEs "has been associated with as much as a 12-fold increase in negative health outcomes in adulthood."*

# *"Awareness of ACEs helps participants change their perspective from, "What's wrong with me?" to "What happened to me and what can I do to rectify it?"*

*Being the innovative and responsive organization that it is, JIT was determined to understand how ACEs had impacted our participants, and I was thrilled to lead that effort! JIT invited participants to complete the 10-question ACEs Survey, and over 300 participants responded.* (pg 70)

*The higher the ACE score, the higher the likelihood of significant disease and disorders. By comparison, 67% of the general population have at least one adverse childhood experience; an ACE score of 6 or more can result in a reduction in life expectancy of 20 years.*

*The JIT results were a loud call to action. **On average, JIT participants scored 8 out of 10, clearly putting them at the highest risk for later negative health outcomes**.*

*In addition to the ACEs survey, we conducted focus groups with participants to identify the difficult barriers they faced while seeking support to heal from ACEs, which included:*
- *Lack of a personal support system*
- *Lack of mental health professionals that truly understood them, their daily lives, and struggles*
- *Mental health stigma*
- *Affordability & Accessibility*
- *Primary focus on surviving, not prioritizing mental health*
- *Lack of awareness of ACEs and their significant impact*

*We learned that other San Diego organizations that provide services to transition age foster youth are aware of ACEs' health ramifications and are using that knowledge to drive their programming and resources, but this important information is still not being communicated to the youth they serve.*

*JIT is the first organization to provide a service that directly informs transition age foster youth about ACEs and their health impacts, while also collectively developing tools to heal from ACEs—including empowering youth to be part of the solution.*

*Awareness of ACES helps change one's perspective from, "What's wrong with me?" to "What happened to me and what can I do to rectify it?"*

*We've learned that a consistent, intimate, healing community is critical for all foster youth. We also learned how healing from trauma is not a destination and it is not instantaneous. Healing is not a perfect journey. In fact, it's not about perfection at all. Healing happens with many small steps and in ordinary ways.*

*I am so joyful to witness the transformational steps our participants have taken to become creative, resourceful, and whole. Not because it wasn't who they were before, but because they now believe it.  - **Vanessa***

Rise to Resilience has been a community approach to health, wellness, and healing that gives permission for youth with lived experience in foster care to be their authentic selves, share their past trauma openly, understand how it impacts them now, and be empowered to determine how to move forward.

This exploration and understanding is accomplished through workshops, group healing discussions, resources, individual and group therapy, coaching and a network of healthy connections— all focused around eight key practices based on healing-centered engagement:

## RISE TO RESILIENCE

 **Healthy Relationships** - Connecting, belonging, needing others, and being needed. The ability to cultivate relationships that provide safety and vulnerability

 **Mindfulness** - Maintaining a moment-by-moment awareness of thoughts, feelings, bodily sensations, and the surrounding environment through a gentle and nurturing lens

 **Holistic Fitness** - Addressing the physical condition of our inner body and emotional state and the role they play in our level of fitness; cultivating a respectful, caring, and appreciative attitude toward the body reflected by sensible health practices

 **Nourishment** – Constructing a nutritional diet that honors the body and gives space for peace and flexibility with food choices; finding enjoyment in eating foods that support sustainable health; developing a healthy connection to the body that notices, trusts, and responds to hunger cues; eating in accordance with our bodies' ever-changing needs; approaching food with curiosity and wonder, rather than fear and rigidity

**Rest & Sleep** – Incorporating physical and emotional rest that restores health and enhances performance; having the ability to cease from the need to be productive; carving out regular time for recharging, recalibrating, and reflecting; enjoying quiet wakefulness and healthy sleep habits

 **Self-Exploration** – Exploring the past, present, and future to gain an understanding of one's true self, no longer at the mercy of inappropriate reactions fueled by inappropriate beliefs and thinking

 **Play** - Taking part in activities that are interactive, fun, and engaging; learning new skills and creating new things; cultivating a growth mindset

 **And, finally, Community** – Engaging in a healing community where there is a sense of belonging that flows from meaningful connections and shared experiences, goals and hope

**Seeing Youth as Creative, Resourceful, and Whole is the Second Choice.**

**What we Build to Support them is next.**

# Choice Two Essential Takeaways

- If we see someone as Damaged and Broken, it puts the focus on **my role as Rescuer, Fixer, and Savior** which may feed my need for significance and being the hero, but it does not support Empowerment, no matter how good my intention might be.

- The Choice to see youth as **Creative, Resourceful and Whole** is to respect their power and wisdom, recognizing their inner knowledge and capacity to make their own life changing choices.

- Sometimes we may need assistance to access our inner wisdom, which is the benefit of the **JIT Coach Approach practices:** setting aside our agenda, being present, active listening, curious questions, and powerful questions.

- Awareness of Adverse Childhood Experiences (ACEs) helps us change our perspective from "What's wrong with me" to **"What happened to me and what can I do to rectify it?"**

- **Rise to Resilience** gives permission for youth with lived experience in foster care to be their authentic selves, openly share their past trauma, understand how it impacts them now, and be empowered to determine how to move forward.

  **Join the Life Changing Movement at jitfosteryouth.org/100KCommunity**

**JIT Staff Creating Community
With the My First Home Moving Truck**

# Choice Three
## *What will You Promise?*

## Build a System or a Community

*Every system is perfectly designed to get the results it gets.*
*A bad system will beat a good person every time.*
                    *W. Edwards Deming*
                    *Management Consultant*

# The System is the Runaway Train

The specific purpose of the Orphan Train was to remove "dangerous" homeless young people from the streets of New York. That mission was accomplished using interrelated social elements working together consistently for decades to relocate thousands of children.

We can assume that Charles Brace and his Children's Aid Society also wanted to help all those young people in some way. But then, as now, we have a better idea of how many children were removed and placed than we do of the "actual help" that was accomplished. The system fulfilled its specific purpose.

**It worked.**

The Orphan Train eventually stopped but, as we've discussed, the system it created persisted and still exists today: remove "at risk" children from failing families, find placements with better families, hope for the best. *Dangerous children* became *children in danger.* In the updated system, children remain *damaged & broken* and the system intended to help them was built on *protection*. In this chapter, we'll explore the fundamental Third Choice to make when addressing large scale problems: the Choice between building a System or a Community.

The profound impact a System can have on the lives of human beings is perhaps best expressed through a story, told by JIT Youth Services Managing Coordinator **Nathaniel Martinez,** who first experienced the foster care system at three years old and then again as a social worker.

## At What Cost?

*My earliest knowledge of the foster care system was when I was three years old. For most of my life, I've had a recurring memory of a conversation during a car ride with my mother. This memory was sometimes so clear and yet sometimes so vague that I found myself questioning its authenticity until I was 32 years old!*

*How well can any three-year-old really remember a single specific conversation? The event itself was so innocuous that it casts doubt on whether it really happened at all. After all, it has always been difficult to pinpoint what about this specific conversation would set it apart from any other conversation a three-year-old has with his mother.*

## "The decision to help, to come alongside someone to address an unmet need, is one of the most profound choices we can make."

*I should also share that this memory has a prologue. I have flashes of being in an office-like setting with a brown wooden bookshelf filled with books. I can see that I'm sitting at a small table meant for children with an adult sitting across from me. I can't remember if this was a man or woman because I am staring down at a piece of paper that I am drawing on. I would later learn that this is a common and helpful tool for this kind of conversation. I would have similar conversations many times with other children decades later.*

*At this point my memory jumps forward to the car ride with my mother. I can hear that her voice is tense as she questions me:*
*"What did they ask you?" I stay silent.*
*"Did they ask you about us hitting you?" Yes, I say.*
*"What did you tell them?" I am silent.*
*"Did you tell them that we hit you with a belt"? Yes, I say.*

*"You shouldn't have told them that! Do you know what can happen if you tell people that we hit you with a belt?!"*
*No, I say.*
*"They can come take you away! Do you want to be taken away?!"*
*No, I say.*

*That is where my memory of the event ends. It wasn't until thirty years later that I learned this conversation with my mother did in fact happen. This was when I formally requested my Child Welfare records from the County and was finally able to get some clarity on these events.*

*Through reading my records, I learned that the person in the flashes of the book-filled office was a social worker and that I had been interviewed as a part of a child welfare services investigation into whether my parents had been physically abusive to me.*

*The investigation was opened after it was reported by my childhood pediatrician that my mother hit me several times in front of the doctor and then took me outside where she struck me over twelve times with her hand within view of the doctor and the medical staff.*

*The notes say that what precipitated these events was my screaming and crying in reaction to getting vaccinated that day. Something typical of almost every three-year-old when it comes to getting shots. What stuck with me most since discovering the details of this incident is that I have no recollection of the event at all.*

*Perhaps it's not surprising because we've learned that human beings do repress memories of certain traumatic events as a defense mechanism. It protects us from constantly being reminded of things that would make it impossible to function.*

I don't remember much over the next few years, but my next memory related to foster care has been permanently seared into my mind. I'll never forget what happened when I was seven years old.

I'm sitting on the living room floor in my pajamas with my mother, my father, and my younger brother. We're watching a movie together when there is an unexpected knock on the front door.

*"I'm then pulled and carried out of my house screaming and placed into the back of a car with two men in ties sitting in the front seat."*

My mother answers and I see a man in a shirt and tie standing in the doorway with two Sheriff's deputies. As they're talking, I can see my mother getting more and more agitated. Voices are being raised and my brother and I are getting more and more upset. I can see the sheriff's deputies push past my mother to enter the house. As the man in the tie and the deputies come in, my mother screams, first at them. Then her attention turns to my brother and me. She yells at us to run.

I can't recall a time where I was more terrified than in this moment. I didn't understand why my mother would tell us to run from the police but the absolute terror in her eyes and voice communicated everything I needed to know.

I quickly run down the hallway to the only place that might be safe and quickly hid under the bed in my room. After more yelling and clattering coming from outside my room, I hear footsteps approach my room and enter. I hear someone calling my name. I can feel my heart beating out of my chest and I can feel myself struggle to catch my breath.

*Suddenly, a hand pulls back the blanket and reaches under the bed to pull me out. I'm then pulled and carried out of my house screaming and placed into the back of a car with two men in ties sitting in the front seats.*

*I look out the window to see my brother also being carried, kicking and screaming, by deputies from the neighbor's house. I would later learn that, as I hid in my room, my little brother, no older than three at the time, had run over to the neighbor's house and was let inside by confused and scared neighbors. Once deputies had arrived and explained the situation, they let them inside to retrieve my brother.*

*With my brother and I secure in the back seat of the vehicle, I see my grandmother pull up in her car. I remember a deep sense of relief as I saw her as the one person on earth that I knew I could count on to always protect me. Surely, she would rescue me from the back of this stranger's car! My relief is quickly met with terror, as I overhear the men with ties and deputies explain to her that she can't take us home with her and that was final.*

*I then remember being driven away as we watched my parents, my grandmother, and my home grow smaller in the distance, eventually fading from view. My brother cries hysterically in the backseat of the vehicle as one of the men pleads with him to stop.*

*After driving for what seemed like an eternity, my brother and I are finally escorted through gates into a room that looks like a cross between a doctor's exam room and a sparsely furnished dorm. We are given gray sweatpants and pullover sweatshirts to wear and sit on our respective beds staring through a small window made of safety wire glass.*

*I would later learn this place was called Polinsky Children's Center, an emergency shelter for children. We did not know it at the time, but my brother and I had just entered the* foster care system and would never again live with our parents. These experiences would profoundly shape the direction of my life and the person I would become.

This is evident most clearly in my decision to first run away from/deny my experience in foster care before embracing it later as an opportunity to learn from and give back to the foster care community.

Turning my lived experience into an empowering experience culminated with my decision to attend graduate school to earn my Master of Social Work degree from San Diego State University.

*Not every child needs to be taken into foster care to be protected. In fact, very rarely is that the necessary or best course of action.*

I spent four years working in the public child welfare system as a social worker, two on the front lines of foster care, conducting child abuse investigations, and two working in extended foster care. That's where I saw firsthand the toll of the systems approach on young people while working with transition age youth, ages 16 to 21, who were preparing to exit foster care.

It was a profound experience for me because, up until that point, I had only known the negative toll that foster care had on me personally. Seeing how it affected hundreds of young people in San Diego truly put everything into perspective for me.

One of the core concepts of the child welfare system is the attempt to balance children's safety, permanency, and wellbeing.

*As a child welfare investigator, you assess each individual family to balance the needs of children to be safe with the need to keep children connected to their family.*

*Theoretically, it would seem simple to keep children safe by removing them from any situation where there is the slightest hint of abuse or neglect. In reality, this approach also comes at great cost to their wellbeing.*

*Not every child needs to be taken into foster care to be protected. In fact, very rarely is that necessary or the best course of action. However, sometimes it is necessary and that's where I saw the conflict between the systems and community approach. I used my own experiences when I was removed from my family to inform how I would balance children's safety, permanency, and wellbeing.*

*I will never forget my experience with one specific family.*

*I was called out to a home to investigate allegations of severe neglect by the parents of five children, one of whom had a significant developmental disability and required much more attention and care.*

*After days of attempted cooperation with the parents, it was clear that they were too consumed by their addiction to address any of the concerns of abuse and neglect that were evident everywhere. The decision was made that the children needed to be removed to keep them safe, giving the parents time to address their addictions and related consequences.*

*It's important to note that while all of this was going on, I was simultaneously investigating over a dozen other families for allegations of abuse and neglect. To put it simply, it would have been easier to simply remove the children and place them either in an emergency shelter, group home, or foster care placement, likely splitting up the siblings into three or more placements.*

*In fact, this is what happens far too often. Social workers, weighed down by oppressively high caseloads and inadequate resources, training, and time, rely on less-than-ideal solutions, often leaving children physically safe (but not always) and at great cost to their potential to have a sense of permanency and wellbeing in their lives.*

*I decided this time would be different.*

*My colleagues and I pooled our efforts to find the children's maternal and paternal grandparents, assess which home could take which of the siblings, create a visitation plan so they could stay in contact with each other, and support the grandparents' physical needs so that they'd have the capacity to care for multiple young children.*

*Once the potential new placements were prepared, we had the grandparents ask permission from the parents to take the children into their care temporarily while we explained to the parents the legal ramifications of having their children removed from their care.*

*In the end, the children had still entered foster care, but there were no police or social workers forcibly removing them. The grandparents gently explained to them that they would be staying with them while their mom and dad got better.   - **Nathaniel***

# The Choice to Build a System

A system is and will always be a poor substitute for the family, a community of caring people, and those lasting connections that children in foster care desperately need.

**A system tends to leave out those who do not fit neatly within the needs and assumptions of that system.**

Every system tends to have certain necessary components:
- A specific purpose it was created to fulfill
- Interrelated elements that work together consistently
- Constraints on how those elements are expected to function

The specific purpose can be innovative, bold, even visionary. In fact, a new system created to solve a problem can change the world in a positive way.

It's the second two components where things get a bit more...fixed.

**A system forms a bureaucracy** which makes the pieces work together consistently but also builds in constraints on what is allowed and what's possible. Individualization hits the brick wall of risk-averse standardization. (Fig. 8)

| Fig. 8 | Bureaucratic/System Impact |
|---|---|
| Hierarchical Structure | Top-Down Decisions |
| Impersonal | Unresponsive to Customers |
| Strict Rules & Policies | Rigid & Inflexible |
| Slow to Change | Lack of Innovation |
| Red Tape | Difficult to Navigate |
| Self-Protective | Resistant to Improvement |

System bureaucracy impedes change. It creates layers of decision-making for every proposed idea. It is internally focused and immune to external influences.

System bureaucracy tends to become rigid and insular. It can be characterized by secrecy and boundaries. It tends to make clear distinctions between insiders and outsiders. It is driven and coordinated from the top down.

**Fundamentally, System Bureaucracy is intrinsically conservative.**

Nathaniel tells us that, for every situation where he tried to implement a community approach within the foster care system, there were several more situations where he simply could not accomplish this with the tools at his disposal. As a result, he simply didn't have the time or resources to achieve his desired impacts, and it became clear that this was a feature of the system, not an anomaly.

Another drawback of the systems-centered perspective is that people become defined by their condition, challenges, problems, or deficits. This approach works well in a triage system, such as in the emergency room during a mass casualty event when it's important to efficiently prioritize the person with the most life-threatening injury. But the approach is no longer effective when applied over a sustained period of months and years as **people are then being *defined* solely by what is perceived to be wrong with them.**

*While the systems approach may appear to be easier to implement and more efficient, it costs more in the long term as these solutions are often inflexible and rigid, leaving people out and causing them to feel unsure, disconnected, and unprepared.*

Within the foster care system, children are often defined by a label in their file, such as the types of abuse they've experienced, their mental health disorder diagnosis, and their behaviors.

This leads to the underlying assumption that children who need help are broken or damaged and in need of someone or something to fix them.

Also, systems tend to be constructed in silos.... distinct parts disconnected and unrelated to one another. So, for example, one system addresses mental health needs and a different system addresses housing needs – with very little communication or collaboration between the two.

While the systems approach may appear to be easier to implement and more efficient, it costs more in the long term as these solutions are often inflexible and rigid, leaving people out and causing them to feel unsure, disconnected, and unprepared.

Even when efforts are made to make a system "trauma-informed," the system approach itself has a gravity that pulls everything back towards the efficient and impersonal.

This is why so many youth exiting the foster care system end up feeling deeply unsure of who they are, unprepared for adulthood and the choices they will have to make, and disconnected from their families and communities.

Finally, in a social services system, there's an established power dynamic in which service providers are in the role of givers and clients are in the role of receivers. A common side effect of this approach is burnout and compassion fatigue.

And when the receivers want to reciprocate with a gift, the system doesn't allow it, robbing the receiver of that empowering experience of "giving back."

# The Choice to Build Community

In a community, there is a give and take. Relationships are reciprocal.

## That's the Third Choice we make.

Just in Time invites participants to join a Reliable, Responsive, Real Community that empowers them to become Confident, Capable and Connected with support that can lead to improvement in any area of their lives. We're committed to providing access to a comprehensive range of services and to seeing the interconnectedness of the strengths and needs of each participant.

This serves two purposes.

First, it's practical and efficient for young people, who are accustomed to being sent from one place to the next, to get their needs met in one place.

*They learn to view their past experience as an asset rather than a liability.*

Second, it communicates to participants that they're much more than the sum of all their problems. They are unique individuals who can become more than they realized and who already possess the wisdom to create the reality they desire.

In the JIT community, we live this truth by consistently declaring that we are all Creative, Resourceful, and Whole.

People are welcomed into the community, just as they are, with no "prerequisites," and are offered opportunities to pursue **their own goals, dreams, and aspirations.**

They learn to view their past experiences as an asset rather than a liability and their strengths as beneficial to themselves and others. For young people in foster care, who've had all semblance of agency taken from them, the opportunity to connect with their personal power and take charge of their own lives can be truly life changing.

To see young people transform their thinking from believing that life "happens" to them to realizing they can do more than they ever thought possible is one of the greatest joys of our work.

In a System, solutions to problems come from the top down - from the experts who've developed a "one size fits all" set of policies and procedures. In Community, high value is placed on lived experience, so it's logical that those who spent time in foster care are best qualified to lead the discussion on how to address their challenges.

When a participant's progress is stalled, they have authentic relationships with caring individuals who are willing and able to empower them to discover their own solutions.

In a System, every problem has an optimal and rational solution that can best serve the greatest numbers of people, which is why systems can be very rigid.
In Community, solutions are individualized. Two participants with similar problems may come to find that their solutions are very different. Communities are flexible.

The end goal is not to find an optimal solution determined by experts, but for participants to lead their own problem - solving and come up with a solution and plan that they feel good about, one that aligns with their values and goals. Only then is it highly likely that they will implement a change and that it will be durable change.

*In Community, it's not simply using more empathetic words or methods to get people to comply with your program. It's seeing one's support role and the role of every member from a completely different paradigm.*

In Community, progress and solutions take time; they are an investment in the future. In Community, it's not simply using more empathetic words or methods to get people to comply with your program. It's seeing one's support role and the role of every member from a completely different paradigm.

In this way, creating Community is a conscious decision that needs to be made every day; and everyone in the organization needs to be aligned to that purpose. There may be times that you fall away from the ideal community you aim for, and that's why it's so important to continually assess the health of one's community by asking Powerful Questions:

1. Are we learning to think differently about who each person is and wants to be, and how each of us can act toward our shared intention?
2. Are we keeping our promise to help and not harm?
3. How can we truly begin to see people and act in a way that communicates that they are creative, resourceful, and whole?
4. What opportunities are there for the people we serve to lead the solutions to their challenges?
5. What opportunities are there for the people we serve to give back to the community?
6. What do the people we serve say about what they need that they aren't getting anywhere else?

7. What opportunities are there for the people we serve to create authentic, long-lasting relationships?

## Other Benefits of Community

Communities are fun!

When you build a community, you have the incentive and freedom to create a space where people want to be.

At Just in Time, we host events and activities where participants, volunteers, investors, staff, and board members come together to recreate, celebrate, share stories, and deepen our connections.

We also create regular opportunities to attain resources, training and education at the same time that we are building lifelong connections.

### Building Community is the Third Choice.

### Who Builds the Community is next.

# Choice Three Essential Takeaways

- **A System forms a bureaucracy** which makes the pieces work together but also builds in constraints on what is allowed and what's possible. Individualization hits the brick wall of risk-averse standardization.

- While a System may appear to be more efficient, the practices are often **inflexible and rigid**, leaving people out and causing them to feel unsure, disconnected, and unprepared.

- System service providers are fixed in the role of "givers," causing them to experience **burnout and compassion fatigue**.

- Community sees the **interconnectedness** of the strengths and needs of each individual; solutions are individualized.

- In Community, **young people transform their thinking** from believing that life "happens" to them to realizing they can do more than they ever thought possible.

- Community believes **individuals are best qualified** to lead the discussion on how to address their challenges, with access to caring adults who are there to empower them.

Join the Life Changing Movement at
jitfosteryouth.org/100KCommunity

95

**JIT Participant Shares**
*Experience & Wisdom at a Community Event*

# Choice Four
## *Where will You Find Answers?*

## Act from YOUR Agenda or Listen to Lived Experience Experts

*Diversity is having a seat at the table, Inclusion is having a voice, and Belonging is having that voice be heard.*
*Liz Fosslien*
*Author*

# Whose Agenda is it Anyway?

In 1853, the answer about what to do with children on the streets of New York came from Charles Loring Brace, who was acting from his agenda: to remove "broken" children from "broken" families off city streets and placed with "good" Midwestern families.

At the time, Brace's Department of Foster Care was a social innovation designed by the day's "experts" with the best of intentions and had a tremendous influence. As we shared in an earlier chapter, his Orphan Train solution affected the lives of 200,000 young people from 1855 to 1929 and millions since, right up to present day.

But what made Brace's agenda an accepted solution?

Was it because he was a Calvinist Minister with experience serving the poor? Or a Yale graduate with a post-graduate degree in Theology? Was it because he tested his idea for years by dispatching children individually to farms in nearby Connecticut, Pennsylvania, and New York, before mounting the first expedition to the Midwest?

Or simply that his idea seemed preferable to the Orphan asylums that were the only "social services" available for poor and homeless children at the time?

Whatever the answer, we can be fairly certain that Brace did not consult with the poor, immigrant families his solution was designed to impact, since his agenda included the belief that they were genetically inferior, a *"stupid, foreign criminal class* and *the scum and refuse of ill-formed civilization"*. *Broken children* from inferior families. *Rescued* from poverty by placements with *better* families so they did not *"swell the ranks of ruffians and criminals."*

98

This *rescue* agenda has been carried on by Child Welfare systems to our present day, implemented by a long-established Bureaucracy that controls and coordinates the elements needed to avoid or minimize risk within a tight web of constraints.

What keeps it intact?

After all, there have been many thoughtful and serious examinations of foster care's persistent problems over the years, from both external and internal sources. Research-driven or experiential insights have been offered by today's accepted experts to encourage change - sometimes incremental shifts and also major innovation to reform, re-design and reimagine established practices. In fact, JIT has benefited greatly from these thought leaders, with increased understanding and capacity to serve.

So, what gets lost from innovative ideas to disappointing impact?

The Experts don't make decisions.  The Bureaucracy does.

# The Choice to Act from YOUR Agenda

Decisions about the fate of a child in foster care excludes their input, no matter their age. As was the case with Nathaniel's earlier story, the positioning of "adult" versus "child" gives power and decision-making authority to those with titles and badges who represent the Bureaucracy. They act on the pre-set Agenda.

Even with limited understanding of a youth, **authority is given to a stranger** acting as an agent of the System to determine the fate of the child.

ssessment of the youth's ability, attitude, and
or is reviewed in a case file written _about_ the youth,
and potentially life changing responsibility.

This practice leaves children in an uphill battle to prove
their worthiness to influence the agenda, both for the short
and long term, regarding decisions that seem small,
practical matters of policy and procedure but can have
lasting effects.

For example, the data might show a successful placement.
Child Welfare Services and the foster care system achieved
the outcome they set out to achieve - success being
defined as a timely placement. Yet, the actual impact of the
decisions on the children and families, positive or negative,
is not known or represented in the results.

## Doing the Best We Can?

With the most important stakeholders (youth and families)
left out of the decision-making process, and their fate
determined by people in positions of power who are
responsible for remaining in compliance with System
policies, practices, and beliefs, "we are doing the best we
can" becomes an all-too-common justification for results
that are not adequate or optimal for those affected but still
fall within acceptable System outcomes.

_A family engaged in the foster care
system is a case. Determining a child's
health and safety is a task._

To **"do what is doable,"** by following a common practice
approved by System experts or conforming to familiar and
accepted policy standards, takes precedence over the
humane practice of listening to and meeting the needs of
the children and families served.

Again, because there is no intention to fulfill an aspirational promise to reach an empowering result, "the best we can" only meets the minimal expectations that have been determined acceptable, even when they are not in the best interest of those being impacted.

That leaves children and families at the mercy of limited beliefs, dated policies, and risk-averse practices that are not youth-centered or family-centric.

Placing children as quickly as possible remains a social worker's top priority: a race against the System's timeframes instead of ensuring quality care; being responsible to reduce caseloads to be ready for the next family, rather than making every effort to meet the individual needs of each family currently under their caseload.

Caseloads are defined by the System/Bureaucracy as "the amount of work (in terms of number of cases) with which a social worker is concerned at one time," the number of cases handled (as by a court or clinic) usually in a particular period.

Synonyms for caseload include workload, load, responsibility, job, assignment, task, charge, onus, amount of work, and commitment.

A family engaged in the foster care system is a case. Determining a child's health and safety is a task.

What could go Wrong?

Ask Just in Time's Director of Advocacy and Community Empowerment, **Simone Hidds-Monroe.**

# What's Easier is Not What is Right

*Entering the foster care system, I was mute.*

*My future was an assignment for a social worker for a particular amount of time.*

*As I was processing the new reality of my life, my mind was foggy and stunned, making speaking an impossible feat. At the delicate age of 13, I had reached the lowest point in my life.*

*The weeks leading up to this life-altering time of my life were filled with the most painful experiences for any child. The strongest person I knew had become so ill and weak that she begged us, her children, to get her to the hospital.*

> *"It was assumed that I was too fragile to be spoken to or to be an active contributor in the conversations of my own future."*

*The battle of her sickness had overcome her poise and control. She was no longer able to hide the pain from her children. It was the first time my mom couldn't do something by herself. She needed help and her children were the only ones there to make sure she got it.*

*Our neighbor rushed my mom and her four children to the hospital. In less than 24 hours, she was admitted, sedated, and sicker than when we arrived.*

*It was the first night in my entire life that my mom wasn't home to watch over us as we slept.*

*Little did I know that this evening would set the precedent for a lifetime of nights without my mother and her protection. There were no words to describe the agony in my heart. A proud and dedicated daughter, now motherless and left to the care of an unfamiliar system.*

*What was there to say?*

*Being mute left me vulnerable to the system. The system had their benchmarks and agenda – to figure out what to do with these four teenagers as quickly as possible - while my nights and moments alone were spent weeping for my mom and the life we were forced to leave behind.*

*My mourning was inconvenient. It was assumed that I was too fragile to be spoken to or to be an active contributor in the conversations of my own future. While the children in my cottage were drawing flowers and butterflies to hang in their bedrooms, I was creating a banner to honor my mom: RIP Edit Eva Johnson, Mother of the Hidds Kidds.*

*Having this banner hung in my bedroom was seen as a sign of instability rather than a small stride toward my own healing. There was no time to process this grief as my future was unknown. Life had to go on. Whether I was ready for it or not.*

*It was my siblings who gave me strength and safety. Our first interaction with the social worker showcases the harsh reality of the foster care system and its harmful impact on children and families. She began our meeting by telling us that siblings, especially those as old as we were, have less than a 1% chance of being placed together after leaving Polinsky Children's Center, the emergency shelter for children in San Diego.*

*This matter-of-fact statistic was appalling and set the tone that this system did not have my family's best interest in mind. The value taught to us by our mom, to stick together no matter what, would be <u>our</u> fight to honor.*

*What further dimmed my light seemed to spark a fire in my siblings. They demanded a different resolution from the social worker. My siblings attended every meeting I had with the social worker to ensure the conversation remained consistently centered on keeping us together and eliminating any possibility of separation.*

*My siblings encouraged me to speak and share my own opinion about a future placement (no matter how long it took) and unapologetically reiterated our family's commitment to stay together. Although I did not always formulate the words, I was aligned with my siblings as they stood up for me and fought for our fate.*

*Who would know what I wanted better than my big brothers and sister?*

*After months of waiting, it came as a surprise to my siblings and me when the social worker presented her 'grand' placement plan for us.*

*"Simone, we believe you would be a great candidate to get adopted. Shane and Clifton, you will be placed in a boy's home together. And Justeen, you are 16, so we just need to find a placement that will accept you as an older teen."*

> *"That day, I made a promise that I would not be complacent, that I too would fight for our fate."*

*All I could remember thinking was, "Who was she talking to? We, the Hidds Kidds, had made it extremely clear our commitment was to stay together. Where was her commitment to seeing this through? Why wasn't she listening? What was influencing this ignorant and inconsiderate plan for my family? Why weren't the voices and choices of my siblings and me being considered?"*

*It was in that moment that I learned 1) our social worker wasn't there to serve us, 2) my silence was not serving me and my family, 3) It was a privilege to be sad, and 4) It was dangerous to be in this system and be silent.*

*Mourning and advocating was a simultaneous dance I had to learn quickly and would be pivotal in my navigation of foster care as a youth and a professional. That day, I made a promise to my siblings and myself that I would not be complacent and that I, too, would fight for our fate. Because the "system" doing their best was not right for me. How many more children were failed by this approach?*

*Special thanks to my siblings – Justeen, Shane, and Clifton for your courage. I love you.* - **Simone**

## Authority vs. Empowerment. Know Your Place

Our current and former foster youth are the experts of the foster care experience. Every policy and practice that makes up the foster care system were lived out by our youth. Every placement that was determined to be a safe place. Every personality they were forced to interact with. Every consequence that was determined to be theirs to experience. Every change made to their lives, whether mandated by the state, county, group home, or foster home, was a lesson that our youth had to endure.

People who work in social services spend their academic career learning the system while our youth spent their lives living it, trying to survive it – which is how their lived expertise developed. During Simone's five years in the foster care system, she was never asked about her thoughts or any feedback on her experience within the system.

She could recite every rule she was expected to follow, name every stakeholder who had power over her life, yet she never considered herself aligned with them.

Her experience in foster care was one of obedience. To keep her family together, to receive all the resources she needed after emancipating from foster care, meant not being labeled a bad kid.

She kept her feedback to herself as she was never invited to a conversation about what could be better. "Be a kid, Simone" was the generic response she would receive from "the adults." Little did they realize that her ability to focus on being a child was forever erased once entering the foster care system.

Instead of honoring our current or former foster youth as the subject matter experts that they are – they emancipate from the foster care system with a "good luck."

For those, like Simone, who dedicate their careers and passions to improving the experience of the current and former foster youth who come after them, they are met with resistance by new generations of adults and decision makers.

As Simone shares, *"We are told our experience in foster care is obsolete, outdated, and does not reflect the experiences of current foster youth. Yet, if the system has improved so greatly and my experience from 13 years ago is irrelevant, then why do the results remain just as devastating?"*

So why not make a different Choice as we build Community?

## That's the Fourth Choice we make.

# The Choice to Listen to Lived Experience Experts

The Choice to empower our young people impacted by foster care is an intentional decision to include them in the decision-making process. To embrace them as leaders and creators of the services and resources they need. (Fig. 9)

From the start, Just in Time's approach has always honored and respected participants' empowered role in their own transformation and encouraged an interconnected/collaborative approach to achieve lasting impact.

Fig. 9 **Foster Youth are the Experts**

**Our Experience is Fact**
**Our Experience is Valuable**
**Our Experience is the Answer**

With lived experience youth consistently holding the majority of staff positions at Just in Time, we continue our successful commitment to utilizing the knowledge of our constituents to evolve our services.

Today with a team of 40+ individuals, more than half of JIT positions are lived experience staff, including the Chief Impact Officer, Director of Operations, Director of Advocacy and Community Empowerment, Key Partnership Manager, Youth Services Managing Coordinators and the majority of Youth Services Coordinators, Volunteer Services Coordinators, Impact Measurement staff, and Development Outreach Coordinators.

JIT staff and participants are integral to every JIT event and communication, acting as lead voices at all significant gatherings.

Building Community as an alternative to System/ Bureaucracy is an opportunity to move away from the traditional power positions as "the all-knowing and all-deciding" to consistent inclusion of the voices and choices of the youth and young adults served.

One of the many beautiful qualities of current and former foster youth is their ability to tell it like it is. When this honesty is met with active listening and humility from people in traditional positions of power, significant improvements and collaborative implementation can produce transformative outcomes.

For any organization seeking this kind of durable change, there are choices to be made – significant, life-altering choices. At Just in Time, we've seen that these shifts in thinking allow innovation that unleashes the power of everyone in our community:

- Youth participants are invited to connect to our community, not "placed" in programs that only meet their most basic needs.
- Youth participants join our community voluntarily as we help them meet their own identified goals as partners in their success.
- Youth participants don't feel the need to distance themselves from their foster care experience but come to embrace their identify as part of a powerful, resilient community.
- Youth participants see themselves as inspirational role models, as exceptional people with bright futures.

- Youth participants take ownership of their story and identity, with a strong internal sense of self and personal power.
- Youth participants create our community as Coordinators, Managers, Directors and Volunteers to keep us honest and effective.
- Youth participants not only "learn how to fish" but join a "fishing village" that they can rely on for a sense of belonging and support.

## A Seat at the Funding Table

In a later chapter, we'll discuss in more detail how creating and sustaining impact has a critical funding component, but we thought it worth mentioning here that philanthropic and government entities can also make the choice to utilize the lived experience lens to decide how dollars and resources are allocated for maximum effect.

It might mean recruiting lived experience board members, lived representation to help determine funding priorities, or having those with lived expertise play a part in reviewing funding applications.

The goal is to maximize our potential for lasting impact by inviting the true experts to influence <u>every</u> decision made on their behalf. After all, they are the ones who will have to live with those choices.

**Listening to Lived Experience Expertise is the Fourth Choice.**

**How we Measure Success is next.***

**\*ALERT - DON'T SKIP THE NEXT CHOICE!**

**\*\* Measuring is VITAL!**

**\*\*\*(Really)**

## Choice Four Essential Takeaways

- **"Rescue" is the legacy being carried on** by our Child Welfare system today, buoyed by a Bureaucracy that controls and coordinates the elements to work together within a tight web of constraints.

- The "experts" don't make decisions. **The Bureaucracy does.**

- **"We are doing the best we can"** becomes an all-too-common justification for results that may not seem optimal for those affected but still fall within acceptable System outcomes.

- Our **current and former foster youth are the experts** of the foster care experience.

- The Choice to Empower our young people impacted by foster care is an intentional decision to **include them in the decision-making process.**

- Building Community as an alternative to System/Bureaucracy is an opportunity to **move away from the traditional power positions** to consistent inclusion of the voices and choices of the youth and young adults served.

- Participants see themselves as **inspirational role models**, as exceptional people with bright futures.

### Join the Movement
### jitfosteryouth.org/100K Community.

**"JIT Shark Tank" Winners**
*Working toward Lasting Impact*

# Choice Five

## *When will You Know You're Succeeding?*

## Report What was Done or Share What had Lasting Impact

*The nonprofit sector is robust and expansive. Lives are being touched every day. Communities are being transformed. But our impact could be amplified if we developed a collective capacity to prove and to improve our impact. We need greater capability throughout our sector for doing clear, deep, and meaningful evaluation.*

*Steve Patty*
*Dialogues in Action*

## Proving. Improving.

Measurement. Evaluation. Data. Metrics.

Okay, let's be honest.  This is **<u>NOT</u>** what you were excited about when you picked up this book.

After all, we're here to do what Steve Patty talked about. Touching lives. Transforming communities. "Heart work."

And how do you collect data on that? How do you measure a person's increased life satisfaction? What's the evaluation process for what happens to the human spirit when there's access to resources for someone who has been in despair?

We **KNOW** that what we do every day is worthwhile. We see it. We hear it. We experience it in so many ways.

Why should you have to come up with some way to take what's NOT a number and turn it into a "metric" to satisfy...whomever?

Why should you spend time and resources counting things that don't really matter to the work you do?

**Great Question.**

Part One of the Answer is: You shouldn't.

Part Two is: The only Data to collect is what DOES matter to you. **The <u>only</u> things to Measure are what truly helps advance your work.**

Part Three is: "Data" is not only numbers.
It's stories and surveys.  Observations, anecdotes, and interviews.

114

It's everything that helps confirm that your Promise is being fulfilled and your Theory of Change is valid.

**Your Data is not for "Them."** It's for you and your team to feel inspired and energized by your success.

## Achieving Impact.

Just in Time's objective has always been to build a long "bridge" for youth after 18 until age 27 as they transition from care with consistent youth-centered support tied to specific intended impacts.

Our Theory of Change suggests that if we assist young people impacted by foster care by helping them become Confident, Capable and Connected, they will also become self-sufficient with a sense of well-being and life satisfaction for the long-term, breaking the cycle of foster care.

Using this foundational framework, JIT created a comprehensive variety of innovative, individualized and volunteer-driven services that met the expressed needs of our youth.

Chances of self-sufficiency increase exponentially when youth have relationships with one or more caring adults, so life-affirming relationships are at the heart of all the work we do and incorporated into all our services.

**But how do we know the impact we intend is actually achieved?**

Most nonprofit supporters, regardless of how and if they express it directly, expect that their support – whether it's time, talent, or treasure - will produce positive results.

That's why, to be sustainable, it's important for nonprofits to track their progress. While the process can be difficult, especially as you move from counting inputs (*how many people we served*) to proving impact (*more on this shortly*), any and all efforts to begin the process increases your measurable benefit and credibility.

It's up to us, the ones doing the work and making the promise, to develop the most relevant indicators that "prove" to stakeholders that their support was justified. The indicators are things we choose to track, producing those key metrics vitally important to us (and those we serve) that will become a scorecard of accomplishments and progress toward achieving our mission.

What's the most effective way to communicate Return on Investment (ROI)?

Generally, it comes down to a combination of Outputs (*the efforts we make),* Outcomes (*the milestones we reach*) and Impacts (*the ultimate destination we hope to reach*). (Fig 10)

---

**Outputs:** What we did    Fig. 10
*Activities (Quantitative):* number of workshops held; number of attendees: number of phone calls, texts sent

**Outcomes:** What happened next
*Effects of Outputs:* number of participants who open a savings account; number who keep and balance their budget consistently

**Impacts:** What is happening over time
*Lasting Change (Qualitative):* percentage of participants who save when finances are tight; who encourage friends and family to save

---

**Outputs:** These are the **Activities** of the nonprofit. For example, in the JIT Financial Fitness services, outputs would include numbers of workshops on smart money management and numbers of connections to volunteer Asset Advisors.

Outputs are Quantitative, tracking "how many and how much," which means they are relatively easy to count. Generally, outputs fill a direct and immediate need. But if the outputs do not lead to any meaningful change or improvement, then the numbers are not useful measurements of progress.

**Outcomes:** These are the observed and proximate **Effects of Outputs**. For example, Financial Fitness outcomes would include the amount of money participants save for a rainy day and any durable relationships they've established with coaches.

Outcomes are more difficult to measure because they require follow-up tracking. "What is different since we began?" is the question that needs to be answered.

The challenge is to draw a credible line from the nonprofit's effort to a significant result.

**Impacts**: These are significant non-observable and internal **Lasting Changes** that can be attributed to the nonprofit's activities. For Financial Fitness, impacts might include durable financial security and sustainability measures, such as investments over time.

Impacts are Qualitative and require the most effort to measure as they require long-term tracking and analysis to make a correlation between the nonprofit's activities and the achieved results. "How has the participant changed for the long-term?" is the question to answer.

# Choose to Report What was Done

So how do you "show and tell" when you're succeeding? Outputs are an easy place to start. You provide a service, count how many attended and how often you provided it.

Outcomes are the next step because they reveal positive effects. They also reward staff, participants, and supporters with a heightened sense of fulfillment.

Fig. 11  **2011 Just in Time Self-Sufficiency Scale**

| In-Crisis | At-Risk | Safe | Stable | Thriving |
|---|---|---|---|---|
| Homeless/ Couch Surfing — **Housing** | Transitional Housing/Dorm < 6 Months | Transitional Housing/ Dorm > 6 months | Has Own Apartment or House < 2 yrs | Has Own Apartment or House >2 yrs |
| No HS Diploma/ No GED — **Education** | Earned HS Diploma or GED | At least 1 yr Post-secondary School, No Degree | Completed 2 years Post-secondary, Trade/vocational | Earned 2 or 4 year College Degree/ Post Grad |
| Unemployed No income — **Employment** | Seeking job or temp, Seasonal Income | Employed in Semi-stable job or Business Venture | 1 yr Stable Employment or Maintaining Business | Permanent and Stable job or Maintaining Business > 1 yr |
| No Budget, No Savings, Often Borrows Money to Live — **Finances** | Unmanageable Budget, No Savings Sometimes Borrows To Live | Budget, Min. Savings Supports self Some of the Time Rarely Borrows | Lives within Budget, Reg. Savings Supports self Most times Never Borrows | Lives within Budget, $3K. Savings Supports self Fully Never Borrows |
| No Connections — **Connections** | New Connections Last 6 months | Consistent Connections in the last yr | Consistent Connections in the last 2 yrs | Consistent Supportive Connections > 2 yrs |
| No Community Service — **Community** | Minimal Community Service 1-4 hrs | Moderate Community Service 5-8 hrs | High Community Service 9-12 hrs | Leadership of Community Service 13+ hrs |

## Looking in the Rearview Mirror

Tracking outputs and outcomes was the starting place for measuring success in the early stages of Just in Time history. (Fig 11) We tracked request types, attendance, distributions, and connections, mostly "looking in the rearview mirror after the fact" to capture what occurred and then adding "snapshots" derived from our self-sufficiency scale.

We soon found that these Outcome "snapshots" gave us only a limited view of how well we were doing.

It was a current picture of how our assistance had helped participants but didn't do enough to measure how well we were progressing from "predictions" of breaking the foster care cycle to actual lasting impact.

# The Choice for Lasting Impact

Most service organizations set aspirational metrics, and their stakeholders expect that those metrics are being tracked and measured. Usually, they can track and measure their outputs successfully.

But is that enough? Our short answer was "no."

The important question is, "What impacts have we achieved?"

And that question cannot be answered by outputs alone.

## That's the Fifth Choice we make.

## Intended Impacts

In 2016, through a grant from The Gumpert Foundation, JIT worked with an organization called Dialogues in Action to build on our Theory of Change and original success measures to set new, clearly defined goals for the future impact we were committed to achieving.

Our intention was for the goals to be ambitious, measurable, achievable *AND* for us to be accountable for reaching them.

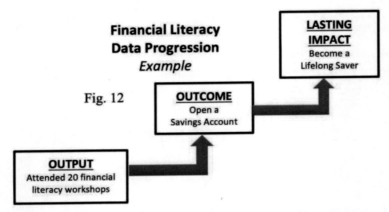

**Financial Literacy Data Progression** *Example*

Fig. 12

One of the key components to measuring our impacts is feedback from our participants. We want to track, not just immediate change or benefit, but lasting impact. (Fig 12)

The question we ask ourselves is "**Are we successfully supporting our participants' efforts to achieve self-sufficiency, well-being, and life satisfaction?**"

JIT tracks these metrics by checking in with participants and alumni through surveys, community conversations (focus groups), and one-on-one conversations. Then services are designed or modified with Lasting Impact as the #1 priority.

But let's view Lasting Impact in the context of a story, told by JIT alumni and Impact & Systems Data Strategist, **James Hidds-Monroe**.

*The day I entered the foster care system was full of confusion, anger, and frustration. My life had changed that day, and I had no control—I felt like I was marginalized and collateral damage for my parents' decisions.*

*I was 12 years old – too young to fully understand why I was removed from my home but old enough for this experience to impact my decisions and interactions with others for decades to follow.*

*I had disclosed to my mother a violent experience I had with my father when he punched me for accidentally breaking a glass jar of pickles. My mother was furious, which was confusing for me because she had also physically hit me as a form of punishment. Domestic violence was a norm in our household, not only towards me, but between them as well.*

*My mother had no idea what to do since she and my father were separated, and she couldn't confront him in that moment. So, she picked up the phone and called the police. When the police arrived, my mother was hysterical and only making the situation worse. Instead of reporting the incident, she argued with them, accused them of being incompetent, and assaulted one of the officers.*

*About an hour after the police arrived, my mother had been arrested and I was sitting in the back seat of a police car on my way to Polinsky Children's Center, a pre-placement facility for new foster youth. I had friends in the neighborhood who were removed by CPS, but I never thought I would be one of them.*

*Over the next six years, I had to learn a new way of living. I experienced a couple of foster homes but most of my time in foster care I was placed in group homes. I became aware of the statistics about adults who experienced foster care and knew the odds that were stacked against me.*

*I remember being referred to as a "delinquent" and told that I would likely end up homeless or in jail. And forget about going to college—nobody is going to pay for it, and only 3% of foster youth graduate with a degree.*

*As an angry teen, I was not optimistic and nowhere near feeling motivated to take charge of my life.*

*Fortunately, there was a turning point for me as I emancipated from foster care, which is when I was connected to Just in Time.*

*At first, I showed up for the tangible things like hygiene kits, bed linens, and dorm supplies. Within the first few months, though, I began to observe interactions that I had never seen before.*

*There were adults who seemed to care about the future of the young people they worked with. I heard conversations that consisted of powerful questions, enthusiasm around each young person's potential, and encouragement for us to actively plan for our futures.*

*"What I appreciated most about the coaching process was that it was on my terms, and it empowered me to make the change I wanted to see in my life."*

*These adults exhibited enthusiasm that was contagious, even for me. Soon, I found that my peers and I were supporting each other in ways similar to how these adults supported us. We were creating a community. I began to envision a positive future for myself. My mind shifted from "I'm destined to be another statistic" to "I refuse to be another statistic."*

*My peers encouraged me to take advantage of additional services that JIT had to offer. Since I had entered college, I signed up for College Bound and was paired with a volunteer coach who shared a lot of the same interests and lived relatively close to me. I joined Financial Fitness so I could manage my finances more effectively. And again, I was connected to a coach who was passionate about financial literacy and had a lot of patience.*

*At first, I struggled to connect with coaches because I had learned not to trust people while I was in foster care. Looking back, though, I'm thankful that over time I was able to have real conversations with healthy male figures about the insecurities I was experiencing.*

*Coaching was different from therapy because I had total control over the sessions. It was new, refreshing, and challenging. In our first meeting, one of my coaches and I created two charts. One was titled **Where Am I Now?** and the other was titled **Where Do I Want to Be?***

*I was challenged to take responsibility for my choices. The coach never indicated what he thought was best nor did he make me feel guilty when I made a decision that others might frown upon.*

*The coach encouraged me to make decisions for myself and not for others. What I appreciated most about the coaching process was that it was on my terms, and it empowered me to make the change I wanted to see in my life. Because of JIT, the resources they provided and connections I made, I know that I'm breaking the cycle of foster care.*

*I'm now 32 years old and I have accomplished so much. I've earned a bachelor's degree, achieved an 800+ credit score, married a beautiful, supportive woman, and purchased a home. - **James***

James' story of where he thought he would be, compared to where he is today, demonstrates the lasting impact JIT strives to make possible for every individual in our community. It's a commitment defined by matching our aspirations to what young people like James **tell us they need,** as we commit to a path to get there together.

## Clearly Defined Intentions

The first step in measuring impacts is to establish Intended Impacts.

That's why JIT establishes these clear goals for every service. Below are two examples.

## Example #1: JIT Basic Needs
**Intended Impacts:**

**1.  Participants cultivate and leverage supportive relationships and networks.**

By this we mean Participants: *have a strong understanding of the importance of relationships and connections to achieve personal and professional success and well-being; become involved in interdependent communities that enable them to accept themselves and embrace support.*

**2.  Participants take ownership of their role in creating positive experiences.**

By this we mean Participants: *gain awareness of their actions and outcomes; are confident in taking ownership of their choices and how these choices affect them and others; practice good decision-making skills and commit to creating positive outcomes; perceive the good intentions of others.*

**3.  Participants make informed and healthy decisions with their money.**

By this we mean Participants: *are able to reflect on their decisions associated with money and the impact on their lives; explore how emotions and coping mechanisms may affect their financial decisions; assess their needs vs. wants; are able to make informative decisions to create more positive outcomes*

## Example #2: JIT Pathways to Financial Power
**Intended Impacts:**

**1. Participants achieve financial security.**

By this we mean Participants: *are able to define and are invested in their own self-sufficiency and path to success; attain the evolving education needed to support their aspirations; develop translatable skill sets; learn and use the most effective methods to acquire meaningful employment; build the knowledge to access essential resources and confidently navigate the workplace; learn and practice effective financial management, including budgeting, savings and establishing strong credit.*

## 2. Participants develop and leverage supportive relationships.

By this we mean Participants: *have a strong understanding of the importance of relationships and connections to achieve personal and professional success and well-being; establish, grow and leverage a network of relationships to thrive; seek out and flourish in interdependent communities that empower them to accept themselves, embrace support, and have the satisfaction of giving back to others.*

## 3. Participants define themselves, their power, and their future.

By this we mean Participants: *have awareness of their strengths and put them to work to overcome obstacles and advance their goals; are consistently proactive rather than reactive; demonstrate personal confidence and resiliency to successfully navigate life's challenges, setbacks and opportunities; develop their personal authentic voice to share their own stories and become effective advocates for themselves and others; establish positive personal habits— physical, mental, emotional—that contribute to long term, sustainable health.*

You may notice that intended impacts may repeat from one service to another. That's because the fundamental empowerment goals remain the same even if the topics differ and, while our participants choose the services and resources that fit their unique needs, it's important that all of the services offered deliver similar empowering impact.

# Deeper. Longer. Powerful. Qualitative Impacts.

Qualitative Impacts measure the achievement of intended impacts. To measure qualitative change, it's necessary to go deeper and to assess internal changes: **Mental, Emotional and Behavioral shifts**.

The **Mental Shift** is from "thinking about something" to "believing it."

The **Emotional Shift** is from "feeling a certain way" to "loving it."

The **Behavioral Shift** is from "doing something differently" to "becoming a different person."

Measuring these shifts allows JIT to verify that our services, resources, and relationships lead to lasting impact.

## The Impact Process: Proving. Improving.

Measurement. Evaluation. Data. Metrics.

The Choice to measure is a starting point for other decisions that lead to more powerful conversations, more strategic solutions, and more confidence in directing resources. More lasting impact.

We know that what we do every day is worthwhile. **The Impact Process helps us decide what to do NEXT.** (Fig 13)

**JIT Org-Wide Impact Measurement Process**

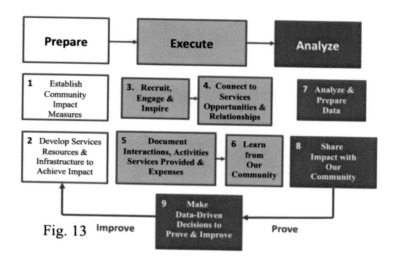

Fig. 13

## Lasting Impact Fulfillment Tracking (LIFT)

For twenty years, Just in Time's Promise for the young people we serve has been to a build a community of support for transition age foster youth where critical resources are delivered through durable relationships to create lasting impact.

In 2020, we conducted our Lasting Impact Fulfillment Tracking (LIFT) survey: 65 questions sent to over 600 JIT Alumni, ages 27-35.

The goal was to explore the impact of our model for building self-sufficiency and stability, well-being, life satisfaction and resilience for the long term.

*Overwhelmingly, JIT alumni surveyed believed they had broken the cycle of foster care with high levels of satisfaction for well-being.*

Life Changing Choices: Just in Time for Foster Youth
Our intention was to determine the key factors that help break the cycle of foster care, then leverage that data to drive future service design and increase impact.

Data was compiled to support analysis of these key areas of interest:

- Current snapshot of **"Self-Sufficiency"** in **Life Success Measures**: *Finances – Education – Employment – Housing – Transportation*
- Current snapshot of **"Well-Being"** in **Life Success Measures**: *Relationships – Healthy Practices – Personal Power*
- Current snapshot of **"Life Satisfaction"** in Life Success Measures

We received 123 responses, 30% of them from alumni over the age of 31.

The LIFT project found several statistically significant factors, answered key questions and suggested service enhancements.

**Overwhelmingly, JIT Alumni (91%) believed they had broken the cycle of foster care** with high levels of satisfaction for well-being.

For those who scored high on the statistically significant indicators of breaking the cycle of foster care, **Relationship Skills** scores were the highest, showing the importance of **being CONNECTED**. This included:

- *Having beliefs respected*
- *Having clear expectations in all relationships*
- *Feeling like a priority*
- *Trusting promises*
- *Being accountable*
- *Being comfortable sharing my inner world*
- *Having people in my life who accept me and make me feel like I belong*

The second highest scores for those who scored high on indicators of breaking the cycle of foster care was in the feeling of **Hope** grounded in their **feeling CONFIDENT**

- *My actions are rooted in hope and optimism and are not rooted in a fear of failure*

The third area of highest scores in those who also scored high on the indicators that broke the cycle of foster care was **Feeling CAPABLE**

- *I build new skills to achieve my goals*
- *I've taken steps to heal my trauma*

*And how did these past participants evaluate the positive impact of JIT on their lives?*

**Major/Life-changing**
| | |
|---|---|
| Housing | 76% |
| Employment | 64% |
| Education | 60% |
| Finances | 54% |

Fig. 14

The data also allowed us to discover that **breaking the cycle of foster care is statistically significantly related to having relationships that satisfy these specific needs:**

- *People who I can talk about my problems with who will help me find solutions*
- *People who support my development*
- *People who encourage my interests*
- *People who it is safe to share feelings with*

Alumni reported high positive JIT impact, with nearly two-thirds saying the impact was life-changing or major (Fig 14). The highest levels of current satisfaction were in the areas of transportation, relationships, employment, personal power, and housing. Some specific results include:
**86%** are employed
82% have stable housing (while 52% of all young adults live with parents)
75% own, finance or lease a vehicle
**87%** have a high or very high level of resilience
**71%** have completed either a 2 or 4 year college, graduate school, or trade school

Life Changing Choices: Just in Time for Foster Youth

We saw that alumni surveyed are successful in life compared to both foster care peers and all young adults, with substantial progress across JIT's successful life components for self-sufficiency, including education, employment, housing, finances, and transportation.

This data was extremely valuable for planning and improvement purposes; we could then double down on what we were doing well and focus more energy on things we could do better for the young people we serve. LIFT gave Just in Time the relevant **Data** that allowed us to go from **Assumptions** to **Verification** to **Action**.

The JIT model had already <u>suggested</u> that by assisting transition age foster youth by helping them become Confident, Capable and Connected, they would likely become self-sufficient with a sense of well-being and life

satisfaction for the long term and break the cycle of foster care.

The LIFT data told us <u>how</u> we meet those needs in statistically significant ways to break the foster care cycle:

- Trusted relationships with staff and volunteers provide participants with the opportunity to work through challenges and arrive at solutions
- JIT services, staff, volunteers, and facilitators support participants' personal and professional development
- JIT peers and the larger community serve as a network of friendly faces to support participants' interests and well-being

With this actionable LIFT data in hand, we determined how JIT could ensure that key practices necessary to break the cycle of Foster Care were consistently employed.

- Provide reciprocal exchanges in all services
- Begin with basic respect for all people and their beliefs

- Outline clear expectations in all services for participants
- Ensure facilitators provide sufficient individual attention so that participants feel like a priority
- Ensure that JIT services empower participants to build new skills to become successful in life
- Create an environment of hope and optimism that encourages growth

We also asked how we could ensure that JIT staff and volunteers always:
- Follow through on all commitments/expectations
- Create a brave place for participants to share
- Hold youth accountable for self-development goals of the services they choose
- Create a space where participants feel accepted and have a sense of belonging

Measurement. Evaluation. Data. Metrics.

It's what Just in Time is excited about because we've seen how demonstrating measurable, lasting impact drives increased support that builds our capacity to touch more lives and transform more communities.

**Measuring and Proving Lasting Impact is the Fifth Choice.**

**How we Sustain Support for our Impact is next.**

## Choice Five Essential Takeaways

- **Most service organizations set aspirational metrics,** and their stakeholders expect that those metrics are being tracked and measured.

- **Outputs are Quantitative,** tracking "how many and how much," but if outputs don't lead to meaningful change, then they're not useful measurements of progress.

- To measure **Qualitative change,** it's necessary to go deeper and to assess internal changes: mental, emotional and behavioral shifts.

- We want to track, not just immediate change or benefit, but <u>lasting</u> **impact.**

- One of the key components to measuring our impacts is **asking the right questions** and by getting feedback from our participants.

- Overwhelmingly, Alumni surveyed in the JIT **Lasting Impact Fulfillment Tracking** believed they had broken the cycle of foster care with high levels of satisfaction for well-being.

**Join the Life Changing Movement at**
**jitfosteryouth.org/100KCommunity**

**JIT Board/Volunteer & Participant**
**Another Story of Lasting Connection**

# Choice Six
## *How Will You Sustain Your Efforts?*

### Follow the Funding or Engage with Impact

**Impact Growth = Income Growth**

*You can't talk about what you're going to do without talking about how to get the money. And you can't talk about how to get money without talking about what you're going to do.*
*Jeanne Bell, Jan Masaoka, and Steve Zimmerman*
*Nonprofit Sustainability: Making Strategic Decisions for Financial Viability*

## Show Me the Money?

Most of us in the nonprofit sector are familiar with setting programmatic goals. For instance, we might set a goal of reducing college dropout rates by 10% in our community or a goal of increasing the durability of volunteer connections.

If the financial goal in a for-profit company is to maximize profit, should our goal as a nonprofit be to have $0 profit? Or should the goal be to grow an endowment of $10 million, or to have a surplus of 5%, or a deficit of no more than $50,000?

# Choose to Follow the Funding

One possible answer is that a nonprofit should have enough money to do its work over the **long term**. The term sustainability is often used for this goal, meaning the ability to generate enough resources to meet the needs of the present without compromising the future, as well as the capacity to develop services responsive to constituencies over time.

This may lead to funding efforts that are essentially aimed at pursuing dollars – the "no money, no mission" mantra – and making promises of results that are outside your passion, expertise, and capacity to deliver.

Sustainability can also sound like an endpoint in itself, a place that once reached would allow the organization to generate financial resources on an ongoing basis. However, what is sustainable today may be unsustainable tomorrow. Funding streams dry up or shift focus, practices evolve, client populations change. But we can always be heading in the right direction.

In fact, we believe there are simply no major decisions that do not have simultaneous, intertwined implications for mission and money.

## That's the Sixth Choice we make.

# Choose to Engage with Impact

Nonprofit emphasis on impacts and on mission alignment is fundamental and aligned with meeting financial goals and strategies. Financial sustainability is not only a legitimate goal; it is a necessary, intrinsic, core organizational goal that involves <u>everyone</u>. (Fig 15)

### Sustainability = Mission and Money

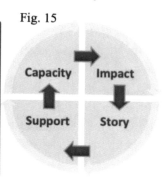

Fig. 15

**Measurable Impact** creates **Compelling Stories** that **Engage Supporters** who **Increase Capacity** and drive **Greater Impact** – a virtuous cycle of sustainability and growth for the Mission.

## NONprofit does NOT mean UNprofitable

Many nonprofits are no longer traditionally funded "charities." We combine donations, earned income, contracts, grants, and other income types.

As a result, different financial goals must be set for different types of income streams, and they must be managed in significantly different ways.

The goal is to develop and communicate an overall strategy that brings together all the activities -- which will have different financial goals -- into a viable business model.

While traditional strategic planning might be likened to looking at a road map, choosing a destination, and setting out on the route, today's continuous strategic decision-making might be more like sailing into the unknown, tacking towards the pole star and changing course as winds and tides demand.

## Invest in Impact

There are multiple definitions of sustainability for nonprofits, such as money, reserves, etc. The Just in Time definition of sustainability is impact-driven. Our belief is that, if you can demonstrate measurable impact, people will be enthusiastic about supporting your efforts.

Measurable impacts provide the tangible proof that our community-based model of support is the answer to the disconnection that plagues so many young people exiting from foster care, resulting in lost opportunities for all of us.

If you can clearly, concisely, and compellingly convey your purpose, you attract funding.

And more money means greater impact!

## Mental Model Shift in How We View Sustainability

This book has shown that there needs to be a shift in the Mental Model to create transformative change effectively and successfully in the lives of young people impacted by foster care.

We would add that a different Mental Model for achieving Sustainability is also needed. It starts with how we think about and talk about our mission and our funders.

## Words Mean Things

At Just in Time, we recognize that our word choice reflects our Intention - how we perceive one another and what is important to us. The word *fundraising* implies that the primary purpose is to raise funds, while *culture of philanthropy* implies that the primary purpose is to build a community-wide foundation of support. (Fig 16)

---

Fig. 16 **Words Mean Things**

CHOOSE common, community-centric language & philosophy

**From Fundraising to Culture of Philanthropy**: Securing resources is not a separate and distinct activity; all staff, volunteers, participants, alumni, investors, and board members are engaged in achieving financial resources, as well as impacts

**From Donors to Investors**: Rather than to donate or "give away" money, the role of the Funder is to "invest" in the mission and those being served by the mission

**From Charity to Nonprofit with a Purpose**: Short-term assistance is superseded by Durable Change

**Ask for Money vs. Invite to Engage in Impact**: The Funder goes from being the "bank" to being engaged in the "solution"

---

The word *donor* implies that the primary purpose of the funder is to donate money, while *investor* implies that the funder's primary purpose is to make an investment that should and will result in a high ROI, a return on investment that truly changes and saves lives.

Merriam Webster defines *charity* as "generosity and helpfulness especially toward the needy or suffering," which implies a short-term solution at best, while *nonprofit with a purpose* implies significant long-term change.

And while *ask for money* implies a polarity, a separation, between the asker and the funder, the concept of *invite to engage in impact* implies that the funder is an active partner in the accomplishment of transformative change.

## The JIT Coach Approach to Sustainability

In an earlier chapter, we introduced the JIT Coach Approach to Communication and showed how we apply those principles and practices to enrich relationships, encourage healing, empower mentoring, and enhance networking.

At Just in Time, we've also adopted those same principles to achieve sustainability. (Fig 17)

## Impact Plus Relationships = Income

In the last chapter, we discussed the importance of measuring and demonstrating impact. Communicating that impact to current and potential investors is a powerful strategy, and it becomes exponentially more effective when combined with Relationships.

Relationships are the foundational key to the success of our community-based model, and they are also instrumental for our sustainability as a nonprofit with a purpose.

# The JIT Coach Approach to Sustainability

**Be Authentic:** Real engagement is the true goal, not seeking dollars. If the engagement happens and deepens – moving from Casual to Connected to Committed – investments in the mission will follow.

**Embrace the Power of Story**: The story we tell is that we are all Creative, Resourceful, and Whole and that our Caring Community transforms lives.

**Seek to Understand:** With every investor, we set aside our own agenda and learn what's important to them. Then we explore how the investor's priorities and passions are aligned with our mission.

**Create the Intention**: Prior to meeting with an investor, we create a Predisposition to set our Intention, including an investor profile, what we plan to accomplish, and flow of the visit. Throughout the visit, we clarify the investor's priorities and goals by using both Active Listening and Curious/Powerful questions.

**Engage the Investor**: We use a one-page Engagement Tool to simply and graphically illustrate:
- The Problem/Challenge/Need We Face
- JIT's Solution to the Need, including Impacts
- Our Primary Priorities
- Our Funding Plan & Needs

**Invite the investor to be part of the solution**: We ask, "Where do you see yourself? Tell me more!"

**Invite Community Connection:** We leverage every opportunity to include Investors in our community activities and events so they can witness firsthand the impacts they make possible

Life Changing Choices: Just in Time for Foster Youth

A community-based, coach approach strategy to achieve sustainability values impacts and relationships equally.

Why?

Because they are inextricably connected. Because, while investors are influenced and inspired by impact, they are most likely to invest in "people" whom they trust and respect.

Relationships are the grease that make the funding engine work. We could share hundreds of examples of how this has been true for Just in Time.

We'll share just one.

## The Million Dollar Meeting

*One of our JIT board members was out at dinner with an old friend when it happened to come up in the conversation that he was a decision-maker for a major foundation. She replied that she was on the Board of Directors of Just in Time for Foster Youth and would he like to have lunch with her and the JIT leadership team? The answer was, "Sure."*

*The JIT staff responded immediately by setting our intention for the meeting, learning about the foundation's priorities, creating a predisposition, and reviewing the JIT coach approach to sustainability to ensure that each of us representing JIT would be on the same page about what we planned to accomplish at the lunch.*

*We began the meeting by establishing rapport and learning as much as we could about the foundation and its leader. Then we used our engagement tool to illustrate our impacts and how they were in alignment with the funder's priorities.*

After we reviewed the "funding plan" at the bottom of the page, where we had outlined how many 3-year commitments we needed, ranging from $30,000 to $1,000,000, the funder looked up and said, "What are you going to ask for?"

Tension filled the air.

All of us looked intently at our CE), who appeared thoughtful and calm. After what seemed like an eternity, he leaned over the engagement tool and pointed to the highest of the funding amounts: $1,000,000

The rest of us could barely breathe waiting for the funder's response.

Ever so slowly, he nodded his head up and down in agreement and then said, "We're going to make the decision in one week; can you submit your proposal and commit to raising at least $330,000 in matching funds within the next 3 months?"

Without hesitation, we said yes. Because, while we didn't know exactly how we'd raise one third of a million dollars in less than three months, we had faith in our community of support. Failure was not an option!

*This first million dollar grant was a turning point for Just in Time.*

History reveals that we were able to write and submit the proposal within three days. The following week, Just in Time was awarded a $1M grant.

At the next JIT board meeting, we shared the astounding news of the game-changing grant, as well as the $330,000 challenge, with our board members.

*Without hesitation, the JIT board chair Brad Livingston stood up and proposed that the board commit to obtaining the matching funds that very evening....and they did!*

This first million-dollar grant was a turning point for Just in Time. We now had significant resources to take us from "survival mode" to big picture thinking, innovation, and new initiatives, ultimately enabling us to deepen our services, disrupt the system, and duplicate our mission by sharing with other communities across the nation.

## The Mission Marriage

The million-dollar story introduces a critical component in the success of any nonprofit with a purpose: an effective Board of Directors.

In every stage of a nonprofit's evolution, the Board can be a source of insight and fuel for innovation by providing strategic leadership, financial oversight, and critical relationship-building. As the mantra reminds us, they provide time, treasure, and talent to sustain and grow the mission for the long-term.

It took just one board member introducing a friend whose foundation had high capacity. Then there was the board chair who quickly rallied the board to commit to the matching grant funds. What was once an aspiration that seemed beyond our grasp suddenly became the new standard for what we could achieve!

At Just in Time, we've learned that each board member needs to have their own "purpose" for their experience to be enjoyable and fulfilling. Their "time" is respected, their "treasure" appreciated, and their "talent" leveraged in ways that have clearly identified impact.

There are numerous books on optimal board governance, so here we'll focus on our key takeaways after twenty years of trial and error. Our efforts were rewarded in 2022 when Just in Time received the prestigious Kaleidoscope Award for Good Governance from the Nonprofit Institute at University of San Diego.

For an organization to thrive, there must be mutual trust between the Board and the Executive Leadership team. It's essential that each board member embrace and live the core values of the nonprofit. And the outcomes are always better when all board members know their specific role and what they're expected to accomplish, with progress and success measured and recognized.

---

### The Three Main Roles of a Board of Directors:
**Purpose, Partnership, and Problem-Solving**

*The Board helps create and advance
the Vison and Mission of the organization*

*The Board is in partnership with the executive leadership
to support the work by attracting resources and
being great ambassadors of the mission*

*Board members are problem-solvers, not for day-to-day
operations, but for Big Picture issues that the
organization may face in the future*

---

Finding effective ways to engage board members and communicate the essential information they need to know can be a big challenge. They're busy people who still need adequate input to make informed decisions, so keeping them in the loop without overburdening them requires a dialogue to strike the right balance. An additional challenge is diversity, not just in gender, race, ethnicity, and age, but in perspectives, backgrounds, and skill sets.

As with all the Choices listed in this book, Intentions need to be thought through and clearly established before you achieve the right mix for the Mission.

Great board members are <u>not</u> simply volunteers with a higher level of responsibility. They hold the future of the nonprofit and the hopes and dreams of those we serve in their hands. Their decisions can truly be life changing choices so it's vital to attract and nurture those who are all in on the Higher Purpose. If you have the right people on the Board, even passionate conflict is constructive and only leads to more creative solutions.

For those conversations, it can be helpful to bring JIT Coach Approach practices into the board room: active listening, curious and powerful questions, and affirmations. As an example, our former Board Chair Brad Livingston replaced the traditional, private "executive session" at the end of our board meetings with "The Good of the Order," when each individual is invited to share a positive affirmation of the work that the board and staff are doing together.

The final three critical elements of effective community-based sustainability are: the Power of Story, the Power of Community, and Extraordinary Stewardship.

## The Power of Story

We've seen that there's nothing more powerful than the spoken word of a participant who has survived childhood trauma and is now on a pathway to healing and success. And our participants tell us that the act of telling one's story is equally as empowering for them as the storytellers.

The challenge is to synthesize all the details of one's life story into a compelling narrative with a theme.

We were fortunate to have a volunteer, Karen Dietz, a Master Storyteller with a PhD in Folklore and Folklife from the University of Pennsylvania, to teach the art of storytelling to our staff and participants. Karen distilled storytelling into three key parts, which we continue to use as a guide for our storytelling today:

- *The problem (specific challenges facing a participant during and after foster care)*
- *The solution (how the JIT community specifically impacted the participant's life)*
- *The overarching message (what this teaches us about the power of Community)*

*Organizations are like people. They do their best when they're connected — to those who care about them and their best interest, who believe in them, and who are committed to their sustainability.*

When shaping a story to tell a potential investor, there are additional points that need to be addressed, including:

- The Why. What is the reason for our existence?
- Where's the money going? What are our priorities?
- How can the investor help to advance their purpose?

## The Power of Community

Nonprofits are like people: they do best when they're connected - to those who care about them and their best interest, who believe in them, and who are committed to their sustainability.

That said, how does a new grassroots nonprofit identify, build, and maintain those connections that are integral to its success?

swer to this question, veteran fundraising expert Andy
ıson shared with us in 2013: "You know everyone you
need to know – right now- to raise all the funds you need."

At the time, that sounded like an outrageous claim. Frankly,
some of us were skeptical, but we respected Andy's
perspective and decided to embrace the notion.

How did we translate this concept into an action plan? We
unleashed the Power of Story and followed our mandate:
Impact + Relationships = Income.

At first, this meant we needed to be out in the Community:
sharing our story and impacts with churches, synagogues,
Rotary, Kiwanis, and women's giving collectives; pursuing
radio, television and newspaper interviews; and holding
salons, which were intimate dinner gatherings at the
homes of friends and supporters.

Over time, JIT developed a series of mission-driven events
where youth, alumni, volunteers, and investors could
gather to learn and to engage, including: our College Bound
event and celebration, the Pathways to Financial Power
Conference and Shark Tank competition, our Rise to
Resilience Mental Wellness Retreat, the Annual Picnic, and
Holiday Parties. Throughout this book, you're seeing
photos of those communal gatherings.

Here is feedback from a new supporter who attended our
holiday party this year: *The opportunity to sit at a table of
wonderful individuals and learn more about Just in Time
through their eyes was very impactful and only exceeded by
the amazing stories of those foster youth that have been
blessed by their connection to your organization. To say we
were significantly impressed is an understatement. We just
wanted to say thank you while it was fresh in our minds—
you all are doing tremendous work and it showed in the
shared stories this afternoon.*

Between March and May, we host Empower Parties at a variety of venues, which serve the dual purpose of creating community connections and raising funds. Each dinner party accommodates 50-150 guests, including two JIT participants/alumni at every table, and lively conversations are supplemented by a short and compelling program showcasing JIT's impact and success stories.

It's an opportunity for board members to share the JIT mission with their sphere of influence and to host guests who are new to the mission.

Connections are deepened and typically over $1M is raised!

In the past ten years, since we adopted Andy Robinson's strategy, our budget increased from $1 million to $6 million, and there's never been a year when we haven't met or exceeded our budget!

## Extraordinary Stewardship

We think it's important to mention one final critical component of community-based sustainability: Extraordinary Stewardship.

It's based on the premise that we have three options:
- Meet expectations – I'm not disappointed
- Exceed expectations – I'm very pleased
- Do the Unexpected – Wow! You really stand out!

Extraordinary Stewardship is "doing the unexpected." It's what makes an experience memorable, builds loyalty, and creates ambassadors. One example is lived experience youth making personal thank you calls to JIT investors. Supporters tell us they're surprised and thrilled when they receive one of these calls, which they say is not a common practice of the other nonprofits they support.

Also, at the end of the calendar year, <u>all</u> JIT staff in <u>every</u> department participate in a massive calling campaign for the sole purpose of expressing gratitude to approximately one thousand investors. That's a culture of philanthropy.

And throughout the year, hand-written cards, homemade videos, and birthday greetings go out weekly. We even personalize every Thank You letter with a handwritten note from our CEO.

At every JIT event, each guest is hosted by a member of our JIT Board of Directors.

Finally, it's JIT practice to respond promptly and proactively whenever a member of our community reaches out to us, even when their request is not related to fundraising or to our mission. We do this because we genuinely care about them and what they care about; we want our actions to demonstrate that we view them as valued members of our community.

## Game Changers, Just in Time

Finally, we'd like to take this opportunity to thank the thousands of supporters in San Diego and across the nation who've made it possible for our impact to grow over the last twenty years.

Below are some of the Major Investors in the JIT mission who've helped us change the world by making Life Changing Choices possible.

They all met our top three criteria for investor recruitment: passion for the JIT mission, capacity to invest, and philanthropic mindset.

## Game-Changers

Aging Out Institute
Alliance Healthcare Foundation
Alta Company, LLC &
    the Grant Family
Andrus Family Fund
Annie E. Casey Foundation
Bank of America
Capital Growth Inc./Art Molloy
    & Dana Worsham
Casey Family Programs
The Century Club of San Diego/
    Farmers Insurance
Scott A. & Elizabeth V.
Christensen Charitable Fnd
Conrad Prebys Fdn
Joan Coppenrath
Greg Cox
Elizabeth N. Crane Foundation
Jeanette Day & Dave Catalino
Deanna & Ted DeFrank
Stacy & Chuck DenHerder Family
Jody Gorran
Walter & Lola Green
Jenny & Tony Hsu
Impact Giving/Katie Milette
Charlie Joyce
Sue & Jay Lichter
Lisa Liguori

Brad & Susanne Livingston
The Livingston Family Fdn
Gretchen & Bill Morgan
Sheila & Dick Murphy
Brad Norris
The Kenneth T. & Eileen L.
    Norris Foundation
Dale Robinette
The John M. Sachs Family
San Diego County Board
    of Supervisors
San Diego Foundation
Satterberg Foundation
SEINT Beauty
May & Stanley Smith
    Charitable Trust
Louarn & Alan Sorkin
Stand Together Foundation
Kathryn Starr
The Swette Family
Rhona Thompson
Tomlinson Foundation
U.S. Bank
Walter J. & Betty C. Zable
    Foundation

## Community Builders

Beck, Ellman & Heald
Chris Burr
The Judith Campbell Educational
    & Community Fdn
Cox Charities
Farrell Family Fdn
Gayle Greenlee
Lori Haynes
Mindy & Peggy Hill
Issa Family Foundation
The Jewish Community Fdn
Junior Achievement San Diego
Kiwanis Club of San Diego
Lily Lai Foundation/George Lai
Lorraine Mahoney & Kevin Byrnes
Laurie McGrath
MG Properties
Jennifer Moores

Marci & Ronnie Morgan
Greg Olafson & Clinton Selfridge
Bob, Suzy, & Lauren Freund
Kippy Gambill
Gesner-Johnson Family Fdn
Rancho Santa Fe Fdn &
    Women's Fund
Judi & Jim Rower
San Diego Women's Fdn
Solana Beach
    Presbyterian Church
Ellen & Bob Svatos
Tina & David Thomas
Sharon & David Wax
Vicki & Jeff Winkelman
Julie & Dale Yahnke

## Honored Supporters

Noemi & Scott Ashline
Shelley & Adam Baker
Laura & Walter Borschel
Inez Branca Family Fdnn
Maren Christensen & Bill Welch
Grace & Scott Chui-Miller
David C. Copley Fdn
Dee & Steve Davis
Day for Change
Del Mar Solana Beach Rotary Club
Lynne & Steve Doyle

Gilbert J. Martin Fdn
Shannon Hagan
Laura Catalino &
    Marc Hoffman
Clarice & Neil Hokanson
In-N-Out Burger
Joe Jordan
Leslie Jordan
Kevan & Mike Lyon
Joanne & Mick Marks
Nordson Corporation
Gillian & George Percy
Bonnie & Jim Porter

# Honored Supporters (contd)

Jeannie & Art Rivkin
Kathy & Dan Roberts
Joyce & Rick Ross
Robin & Larry Rusinko
Dr. Ruth & Gary Samad
Mark Schmidt
Dave Schulman

SDG&E/Sempra
Barbara & David Snodgrass
Mike Stivers
Tuffli Foundation
Dr. Renee Wailes
Sandra & Peter Zarcades

And special thanks to these individuals for their wise counsel and friendship throughout the years:

- The JIT Co-Founders Jeanette, Louarn, Kathryn, Tony, and Jenny who led with passion and heart

- Founding Members, including Elizabeth Dreicer, Phil Baker, Lisa Foussianes, and Dr. Patricia Benesh whose unique talents furthered our mission

- Alan Sorkin, whose wisdom shone a light on our path

- Marty Goodman and San Diego Social Venture Partners, who opened doors and challenged us to grow

- Linda Spuck and Nancy Spector, who guided us through the maze of Legacy Giving

- Mike Gemm, who helped us find "a handful of people"

- Dr. Richard Levak, Linda Rock, and Bill Morgan who forged a partnership with local universities to offer robust mental wellness services

- Claudia and Arthur Schwartz, who expanded our reach thru Coaching & Network

- Ted DeFrank, who urged us "not to sweat the small stuff."

- Tireless mentors and connectors, including Diane and David Archambault, Lauri and Steve Buehler, Grace Chui-Miller, Gretchen Morgan, Suzy & Bob Freund, Val Sussman, Rhona Thompson, Pierre Towns, Sam Webster, and so many more

- Brad Livingston, whose Vision set our course: *"We're changing the World....one Youth at a Time!"*

## Engaging with Impact is the Sixth Choice.

## Choosing to Act is next.

# Choice Six Essential Takeaways

- Nonprofit emphasis on **impacts and mission** alignment is fundamental and aligned with meeting **financial goals and strategies**.

- If you can **demonstrate measurable impact**, people will be enthusiastic about supporting your efforts.

- A community-based, coach approach fundraising strategy values **Impacts and Relationships** equally.

- Organizations are like people: **they do best when they're connected** - to people who care about them and their best interest, who believe in them, and who are committed to their sustainability.

- There needs to be **mutual trust** between the Board and the Executive Leadership team.

- Outcomes are always better when all **board members know their specific role** and what they are there to accomplish, with a way to measure their progress and success.

- Use the power of **Story and Community**.

- Rather than focus on asking for money, **invite the Investor to engage** in the mission.

- **Extraordinary stewardship**: Do the Unexpected.

**Join the Life Changing Movement at jitfosteryouth.org/100KCommunity**

**Making Life Changing Choices in Santa Clarita**
*Fostering Youth Independence*

# Choice Seven
## *Who Can Start THIS Where You Live?*

## Wait for Someone Else or
## Be the Needed Change

*You must be the change you wish to see in the world.*
*-   Mahatma Gandhi*

## Somebody Should Do Something

It all started with gift baskets.

As Diane shared earlier, during the 2002 holiday season two women delivered Christmas gift baskets to 25 newly "emancipated" young people living alone in subsidized and often empty apartments. The women were both inspired by the spirit of these 18-year-olds and horrified by their circumstances.

They had two thoughts. First, "This is just wrong!" And second, **"We can and should do something about it."**

This **MITTCE** (remember, Moment in Time That Changes Everything?) led to the birth of Just in Time for Foster Youth and 20 years of impact on the lives of thousands of young people.

Some might think that change depends on "leaders" who have some special quality that gives them the ability to create movements. Someone once said, *"If your actions inspire others to dream more, learn more, do more and become more, you are a leader."* This was the case of the Just in Time founders. They became leaders because they chose to help youth, not because they thought they were blessed with some extraordinary ability to lead.

# The Choice to Wait for Someone Else

So, what keeps us from taking action?

Taking the lead is both scary and difficult. There's a fear of failure, of not having what it takes to win the day, of disappointing those you ask to follow.

158

It's true that leadership for change does take some courage. In fact, all leadership is about being willing to step into the uncertain and the unknown as an act of faith. As Dr. Martin Luther King said, "Faith is taking the first step when you can't see the whole staircase."

**The Choice to Wait is to accept the current reality.**

# The Choice to Be the Needed Change

Someone has to make the Choice to push through doubt and fear to overcome big obstacles.

The Question becomes *What Would You Do IF You Knew You Could Not Fail?*

In the beginning, it may just be about Inspiration. You share your Dream with others and persuade them to take a leap into the unknown. You have a Vision for how to make something better, but you need others to follow you and help make it happen.

*What would you Do if you knew you could not Fail?*

So, you act as a torchbearer, illuminating the path from here to there by helping them understand where they're headed and what the journey ahead will look like. You describe your vision vividly and compellingly so that your fellow travelers long to see it become a reality.

To move forward, you encourage people to assume new goals and responsibilities. That's not an easy task.

People will often reject something that rocks their world, so you must paint a compelling picture of the rewards they'll gain to entice them to jump in. Show them that the rewards justify the risk.

The middle, as in any good novel or movie, is where most of the tension plays out — the scrappy fight, the steep climb. Challenging the status quo does not come without hardship. Complex processes may prove more difficult to simplify than anticipated.

It's your job as the leader to remind people what's at stake and encourage them to press on. Overcoming hurdle after hurdle can dampen everyone's enthusiasm.

For this reason, you need to reenergize people by acknowledging the progress they've made. Remind them of key milestones and celebrate small wins while keeping their sights set on the Big Goal.

In the end, you and your fellow doers arrive at the new destination. When the dream becomes reality, everyone deserves (and needs) a victory dance!

Whether big or small, this "movement" has changed the course of the future. It's also time to take stock of lessons learned to prepare for the next journey, because if you're planning to stick around, you'll soon have another dream. And another.

## Fostering Youth Independence

As JIT celebrates our 20th Anniversary, we're committed to fulfilling that aspirational Vision of "scaling by sharing" our transformative model for relationship-based services and resources led by and for youth with lived experience in foster care. By this we mean that we invite other cities, counties, and states to benefit from the JIT model, and we offer our assistance in adapting our model for their needs.

Six years ago, we partnered with a group of volunteers from Santa Clarita, California, who visited us in hopes of duplicating JIT's approach. Five years later, **Fostering Youth Independence (FYI)** has served over 140 young people and is building a reliable community of support for years to come.

**Carolyn Olsen**, co-founder of FYI, shares their story.

*I was introduced to the foster care system about ten years ago, when I became friends with Gina Stevens. Gina and her husband were fostering two teenagers, and Gina would share some of the needs and challenges their foster youth faced as they transitioned to adulthood.*

*A few years later, in 2016, I had the opportunity to volunteer as a CASA (Court Appointed Special Advocate.) I learned about the foster care system by immersion as a I met with social workers, spent hours in dependency court watching a bureaucracy attempt to parent children, and developed a relationship with a 17-year-old girl living in a group home who had endured more trauma in her young life than anyone I've ever known.*

*"It became clear to me that money alone was not the answer; foster youth needed people who cared."*

*The first time I met her, she shyly told me that she wanted to go to college, but she had no idea how to go about it. I began doing research and learned that there was a wealth of financial aid available to foster youth, but without assistance and encouragement from a knowledgeable adult, the process of applying for it was overwhelming.*

*It became clear to me that money alone was not the answer; foster youth needed people who cared.*

*Gina and I began to have conversations about how we could engage our local community in Santa Clarita, California, to support aging-out youth. We were both long-term residents of Santa Clarita and were convinced that people would help if they only knew about the need. We briefly tried to start a program at a local church but found that we lacked the autonomy to provide the kind of help we thought was needed.*

## *"We decided that our mission would be to equip foster youth to complete a post-secondary education and become successful, independent adults."*

*As we were leaving a somewhat frustrating meeting, Gina turned to me and said, "We should start our own program!" And so, it began.*

*Soon, our friend, Stacey Anton, a former public health nurse who had worked with Child Protective Services to serve chronically ill foster children, learned about our plans and offered to help. We believed that, if we could change one life, it would be worth it.*

*In January of 2017, Gina, Stacey, and I began meeting regularly to flesh out our plan. Convinced of the difference a dedicated, caring adult could make in the life of a foster youth with no family support, we developed the concept of a volunteer Ally, a caring adult who would provide the one-on-one support, guidance, and assistance each foster youth needed.*

We reached out to other professionals for guidance and feedback. I met with Dora Lozano, the foster youth liaison at our local community college, College of the Canyons, and asked her what she thought of our idea. She could not have been more encouraging, and we went on to develop an amazing partnership!

We talked to Amy Lemley, Executive Director of John Burton Advocates for Youth. As we discussed all the ways we wanted to help, Amy encouraged us to hone our mission. She shared that, for foster youth, a post-secondary education was the difference between poverty and the middle class.

We decided that our mission would be to equip foster youth to complete a post-secondary education and become successful, independent adults.

My husband did a Google search and found an organization in San Diego that was doing what we wanted to do. Don Wells and Diane Cox of Just in Time for Foster Youth agreed to meet with us and share their experience. Don and Diane became our mentors, providing invaluable advice and encouragement.

Gina and I then met with the leadership of the Santa Clarita DCFS (Department of Children and Family Services) office, who excitedly affirmed our plans. Lacking the legal qualifications to start a nonprofit, we presented our vision to family law attorney Tess Cozine, whom Gina had met through her foster youth.

Tess enthusiastically responded by donating her time and expertise to file the new organization's articles of incorporation, write its bylaws, and become a member of our founding board of directors.

*We wanted the organization to have a name with an acronym or abbreviation that youth and supporters would remember.*

*BFF and LOL didn't work, but FYI was catchy, and **Fostering Youth Independence** represented our mission. Our talented friend, graphic designer Kate Pitner, donated her time and talents to design FYI's logo.*

*I filed for and obtained tax-exempt status, and we opened a bank account and started receiving donations. Stacey's neighbor volunteered to be our bookkeeper. Meanwhile, Gina and Stacey were working on the youth intake and Ally training processes.*

*Through our connections with our community college foster youth program, we met a brave young lady, Tiese, who agreed to be FYI's very first participant. (She eventually became FYI's first student to earn her bachelor's degree!) With Tiese's help, the intake process was developed.*

*Gina and Stacey also spent hours researching trauma and its effects, and together they developed our volunteer training program. We began doing community outreach, recruited our first volunteer Allies and held our first training session. We checked references, conducted interviews, Live Scanned, and welcomed a team of people who would invest their time in foster youth.*

*Every time we reached out for help, our community met the need.*

*FYI received youth referrals from Dora Lozano and DCFS, and Gina and Stacey did intakes and started pairing youth with Allies.*

*In August, FYI held its first Back-to-School event with 9 youth!*

And then, we started to see the difference that a caring adult and a nurturing community could make in the life of a young person exiting foster care.

We never imagined the outpouring of support we would receive. Every time we reached out for help, our community met the need. A local church donated our office space. Other churches supported us financially. We applied for and received grants from the City of Santa Clarita.

Family and corporate foundations generously funded weekend empowerment retreats, emergency financial needs, events, and more! Local organizations like Zonta, Assistance League, Rotary Club, Santa Clarita Runners Club and Soroptimists met a multitude of needs.

A local couple purchased a property to house 4 of our youth at a rent they could afford. Individuals and churches donated backpacks and duffle bags, bikes and cars, sleeping bags and camping supplies, hygiene items and school supplies. Others sponsored holiday wish lists, made stockings and donated holiday pajamas and stocking stuffers. Many answered our appeals for financial support and gave generously so we could meet youth needs.

## "FYI has been successful because we know our community, its resources and services, its churches and organizations, and its people!"

Over 100 people have volunteered as Allies, and we have watched youth blossom as their Allies encourage and care for them. Allies have been there for youth during good times and bad times, attending graduations and celebrations, and showing up at accident scenes and hospitals, too. One Ally even walked her youth down the aisle at her wedding!

*A retired LCSW serves as our mental health consultant and leads our bimonthly Ally support groups, called "Coffee & Conversations."*

*Other volunteers have served as event coordinators, office administrators, birthday card coordinators, intern supervisors and volunteer coordinators.*

*Thanks to our amazing community, FYI has been able to provide 140 current and former foster youth with the hope and guidance they desperately need and deserve! As a result, 24 youth have graduated from high school, 18 have earned associate degrees, 5 have completed trade programs, and 8 earned their bachelor's degrees! Forty-four youth have secured stable housing, and many have obtained driver's licenses, gotten jobs and taken other strides toward independence as a direct result of the support they received from FYI.*

*But most importantly, 140 youth know that they are loved and that they matter.*

*We are often asked if we plan to open FYI chapters in other locations, and our answer is "no." FYI has been successful because we know our community, its resources and services, its churches and organizations, and its people! We love being a local nonprofit that engages its neighbors to help those in the community. However, we would be thrilled to help others start their own programs where they live.*

*If we all do our part, we can achieve our vision: a future in which every youth leaving the foster care system feels safe, connected, and loved.  - **Carolyn***

## How <u>We</u> Can Help, Just in Time!

When we started this journey with you at the beginning of this book, we said Nyla was the reason we wrote it.

We also wrote it for the thousands of young people, **our** children, both in and out of foster care across the country, who need us all to make different choices.

Just in Time is committed to expanding our impact nationally by utilizing the **three "scaling by sharing" options** below rather than attempting replication.

As Carolyn said, we want to empower communities who are "experts" in their local capacity and available resources, inviting them to utilize the JIT model we've shared in ways that fit where they are and enhance their existing focus.

**Scaling Influence (as a Field Builder/Thought Leader)** means helping others to understand and adopt the JIT mental model: community-based, individualized, youth-centered, and lived experience-driven services and resources. This means a fundamental shift in traditionally unexamined paradigms that result in "unconscious" resistance to system change. It requires building awareness, networking, and access to decision makers.

*Our Big Hairy Audacious Goal is lasting impact for 100,000 young people who are impacted by foster care nationwide, a "100K Community" within 10 years.*

**Scaling Capacity (as an Accelerator/Partner)** means hands-on consulting with organizations to maximize elements of measurable impact, sustainable finances, effective staff/culture, strong infrastructure, and compelling marketing. It requires a dedicated, empowering JIT staff.

**Scaling Implementation (as a Tool Provider/Coach)** means sharing various unique JIT services such as Financial Fitness, Rise to Resilience, College Bound and the Coach Approach training that maximizes staff and volunteers to become powerful partners for the youth they touch.

Just in Time's **Big Hairy Audacious Goal (BHAG) is lasting impact for 100,000 young people** who are impacted by foster care nationwide, a "100K Community" within 10 years, achieved by partnering with organizations across the country who will share our proven theory of change. By our calculations, 100K is 50% of the 200K transition age youth, ages 18-27, who reside in the U.S.

This establishes the "specific goal" key element of our Big Bettable Promise and gives us a powerful vision for partners, potential funders, and influencers who might share our ambitious scope of work, inviting others to play significant parts in scaling systemic change.

The Impacts we aim for as we scale up will fall into several categories and will be customized based on the option and the partner. However, a community base and focus will be the constant thread for success.

First, we'll measure/track our influence as we are invited to forums, serve on collaborative groups, create ongoing partnerships with organizations that align with JIT's mission and vision, and garner regional/national attention for our model. This will be more of a leading indicator of impact.

Second, we'll measure/track our impact on the organizational level regarding the adoption of our relationship/community model. Are organizations utilizing volunteers as durable relationships? Have they hired lived experience youth as staff/leaders? Have they adopted the Coach Approach model for volunteer training? Are they tracking self-sufficiency and well-being?

An empowered, energized, extraordinary 100K Community that all started with 25 gift baskets.

**What would YOU do if you knew you could not fail?**

**That's the Final Choice.**

## Choice Seven Essential Takeaways

- **In the beginning,** you share your dream with others and persuade them to take a leap into the unknown.

- **The middle,** as in any good novel or movie, is where most of the tension plays out — the scrappy fight, the steep climb.

- **When the dream becomes reality,** everyone deserves (and needs) a victory dance. Whether big or small, this "movement" has changed the course of the future.

- <u>YOU</u> **can do it!** Groups like Fostering Youth Independence and Just in Time for Foster Youth have shown it can be done.

- Just in Time is ready to partner to impact nationally, utilizing three **"scaling by sharing"** options, rather than replication, so that other communities can utilize the JIT model in ways that best fit and enhance their existing focus.

**Join the Life Changing Movement at
jitfosteryouth.org/100KCommunity**

JIT Participants & Volunteers

# Part 3

# The Choice to Fail Our Children

## *"The Family I Always Dreamed Of"*
# Victoria's Story

*My first, REAL family-oriented foster care placement was when I was five years old. There was both a mom and a dad present. I had a brother and sister who I connected with very well.*

*As a family, we would get dressed in nice clothing and go to church every Sunday. If my siblings and I did well in Sunday school, we would all go out to eat at my favorite Chinese buffet. I remember going on trips and different outings and, although I joined their already established family, I didn't feel like the outcast. To me, this is what family should be.*

*Just when I thought I was comfortable in a stranger's home and enjoyed life, once again, another placement. Only this time I didn't see a reason for it. I was fed three times a day and the roof we lived under didn't have a 30-day notice on it. I didn't know why I was being transferred but, as a minor, I had ZERO say.*

*There was an immediate change in family dynamics. Instead of living with a mother, father, brother, and sister, I was placed in a home that included a grandmother, her daughter, adopted grandchildren, and day care kids. To me this was a true foster home. I felt disconnected and displaced.*

*My biological mom was released from prison around my sixteenth birthday, and this time she seemed stable. She saved enough money to rent a studio apartment and I was desperate to try to make our family normal. I knew she didn't have a job and couldn't keep up with rent, but the idea of waking up next to the woman who gave me life was worth the risk. My dad popped up one day and I was sure I could now mirror my first foster family.*

*Unfortunately, my parents backslid into their bad habits, and I found myself waking up and going to bed alone.*

*My parents were gone days at a time, but I believed deep down they would come home to the daughter they claimed they would do anything for.*

*After trying to provide and care for myself while still in high school, I realized I had to give up on this mommy-daddy-daughter fantasy and my only option was to go back into foster care. I moved a few more times before my senior year. I was tired of changing and moving. I felt like I was owned by the system. Whenever they said move, I moved. I felt obligated to conform to each placement although my heart didn't want to.*

*Consistently having to alter my identity to please my caretakers, I found myself completely losing myself. I knew school was the only route to having any future of my own. I spent late nights and early mornings in the career center because I was determined to go to college even though I didn't know where to start. Fearful that I would not be admitted to a four-year university, I applied to a total of fourteen schools. None of this was easy. But I accepted the fact that I would have to work twice as hard because there was no plan B.*

*To my surprise, I was accepted into my dream school and now alma mater, San Diego State University, which at the time, had a 23% acceptance rate.*

*While I was in college, Just in Time became the supportive family I always dreamed of having. When I was moving into my dorm, I didn't have the necessities and JIT was not at all hesitant to step in. I received a laptop, printer, and $350 dollars to furnish my dorm.*

*This was the mere beginning of what JIT would do for me over the next few years.*

*One of the recent JIT services I participated in is JIT Shark Tank which promotes and supports former foster youth in entrepreneurship. I partnered with another mentor who helped me build a business plan which we submitted to a competition to win $5,000 towards my business. We did it!! I won the competition and was able to purchase digital equipment to start a podcast that dives into the experiences of entrepreneurs in Southern California!*

*Through JIT, I found a community of loving support including Karen and Dale Miller, a couple who have welcomed me into their home and accepted me as their own. They are the reasons I now can say I've studied and lived abroad in Murcia, Spain where I also had the opportunity to travel to a total of 26 countries.*

*My greatest feeling of gratitude and self-worth came when I started to share my story with the intention of spreading the awareness of foster care. I received so much love, gained support from dozens of community members and, to this day, my possibility and opportunities seem endless!*

*Looking back, sharing my story has been extremely impactful to myself, my audience, and all the former foster youth JIT is currently supporting. I truly believe I could not be who or where I am today had I not encountered JIT; they have opened so many doors for me and I am eternally grateful. -* ***Victoria***

# America, We Have a Problem... and We Also Have Choices

*If you do not change direction, you may end up where you are heading.*

*Lao Tzu*

*Do or do not. There is no try.*

*Yoda*

# What happens if we <u>don't</u> act?

So here we are, at the end of <u>this</u> part of our journey.

Our intention has been to share lessons we've learned to start a conversation with people we haven't yet met to change how we see and respond to young people in our communities who have been neglected for far too long.

We believed we could take what might seem a complex and persistent challenge and offer a clear foundation for taking action to empower Life Changing Choices across this country.

We know there's no guarantee that anyone will join this "Just Cause." We also know what to expect if we don't change our Choices.

**We'll repeat the numbers again because they need to change.**

In 2021, 19,130 youth emancipated from foster care: 46% white, 21% black, 21% Hispanic, 12% mixed or other (*AFCARS*)

Research shows that one in ten will have a child between ages 17-19, with one in four having a child between 19-21. (*AECF - Annie E. Casey Foundation*)

About 1 in 4 youth who age out of the system will not graduate from high school or be able to pass their GED. (*NFYI*)

More than 60% of child trafficking victims are current or former foster youth (*NFYI*)

Only 50% of foster youth who age out of the system will have some form of gainful employment by the age of 24. *(NFYI)*

Only 6% of those who age out of the system will attend an institution of higher learning and only 50% of those will be able to graduate with a degree *(NFYI)*

The American Academy of Pediatrics Healthy Foster Care American Initiative identifies mental and behavioral health as the "greatest unmet health need for children and teens in foster care." Up to 80% of children in foster care have significant mental health issues, compared to approximately 18-22% of the general population. *(NCSL)*

Not only is this a tragic loss of human potential, but for those who are more financially focused, our economy pays a heavy price later for underinvesting in foster children.

- If aged out foster youth had the same outcomes as youth who didn't age out, US taxpayers would save $4.1 billion *(Finally Family Homes and attributed to AECF)*
- On average, for every young person who ages out, taxpayers and communities pay $300,000 in social costs over that person's lifetime. 26,000 young people aging out x $300,000 per person = $7.8 billion in total cost *(NFYI)*
- 75% of women and 33% of men receive government benefits to meet basic needs after they age out of the system. *(NFYI)*
- Within four years of aging out, 70% will be on government assistance (iFoster)

None of these outcomes just happen.

They result from many factors, including our lack of knowledge and understanding of foster care, faulty mental models designed to keep foster youth out of sight (just as the Orphan Trains helped children disappear from New York streets), and our tendency to believe that "someone else" will take care of the "problem."

The truth is that our Choices have had devastating consequences for the young people who continue to be placed on a track that leads to despair, anxiety and a cycle that can be broken if we decide to do it.

**When will we Choose to get off the Orphan Train?**

# How Can We NOT Do What's Needed?

We started this book with Nyla and now we'll end with **Caitlin**, a Just in Time alum who is now our Key Partnerships Manager.

Caitlin will make our Final Call to Action... an invitation to make your own Life Changing Choices.

*People intend to keep the promises they make, then life happens. As much as we hope that everything will be OK, there's always mitigating factors that alter the circumstances.*

*Making a commitment to care for a child is, from the perspective of the child, much like a promise. Unfortunately, promises broken in foster care can be profoundly life-altering. And with every broken promise, a child grows up a little faster, more jaded and hurt. With every kept promise, they can heal.*

*What will you promise?*

*The average well-intentioned and caring adult could see a complex problem, like thousands of unaccompanied children running the streets and think, "Let's build a system to solve this huge problem." Millions of dollars and working hours could be poured into this "system" to remedy the problem.*

*Yet for some reason the system makes the problem worse, and the problem is never solved. In the foster care and juvenile justice system, children are separated and isolated, assigned numbers and labels, diagnosed and medicated, silenced and exploited, and moved around until they age out.*

*This system and the people that operate within it approach each unique child and family with uniform legal practices facilitated by law enforcement, officers of the court, and social workers. There is a disconnect between all parties, the needs of the child and family are left unmet, further trauma occurs, there is no accountability, and, in time, another youth ages out of the system to end up homeless or in prison with their own children falling into the same cycle.*

*This system fails young people, and we allow it.*

*Well-intentioned and caring individuals look at the system and think, "Let's fix it!" They might invest thousands of dollars and hours of study into a college degree to become a social worker and remedy the problem. Yet for some reason their life's work only perpetuates the same broken system and the problem is never solved. Because the foster care and juvenile justice systems are intertwined and rooted in colonialism, racism, and oppression.*

*I dream of a revolution where the entire system is done away with.*

*In communities, on the other hand, people can come together to help one another, to hear each other, and to heal. In communities, we can create the village that raises the children, build relationships, stay connected, and garner the needed resources. For me, the difference between systems and communities is life and death.*

*Finding the Just in Time Community has been life changing for me. Initially, when I heard a radio commercial inviting former foster youth to visit JIT, I expected a resource hub for food banks, housing waitlists, and free wi-fi. Discovering a community of support made up of my peers, caring adults, mentors, coaches, and allies has empowered me and changed the entire trajectory of my life.*

*By being part of a community, I've learned that I am creative, resourceful, and whole. I've gained the confidence to face my fears, follow my heart, use my brain, and reach my full potential. I've made connections with people from all walks of life who are committed to something bigger than themselves.*

*Because of this community, I know I am capable of anything, and every young person in care should know that, too.*

*As a lived experience staff member at Just in Time for Foster Youth, the work I do connects people of different generations and economic circumstances on a level playing field where they can see we are all creative, resourceful, and whole.*

*In a room full of affluent do-gooders, I am the unapologetic voice advocating for my peers. I open their eyes to the struggle and encourage them to mobilize future progress.*

*As a former foster youth, I'm very proud to use my time and talents to serve the remarkable and resilient young people in our community.*

*Recently, with the launch of the JIT Network, we've been able to connect foster youth and allies across the nation. With the intention of connecting 100,000 youth who've been impacted by the foster care system over the next 10 years, we're creating a responsive, reliable, real community that can truly break the cycle of foster care.*

*With lived experience leading the discussion, we're identifying the problems, analyzing the root causes, making demands, and waging our campaigns! As thought leaders in the space of empowering young people, we're disrupting the system and addressing systemic issues that cause barriers for former foster youth to thrive.*

*We're providing services and resources through a community-based model that allows youth to participate in their own healing journey and make their own life changing choices! -**Caitlin***

**Our children are waiting for us to make different choices.**

# What will <u>you</u> Choose?

## A Final Call to Action

**CHOICE ONE:** Prioritize Empowerment

**CHOICE TWO:** See Creative, Resourceful, & Whole

**CHOICE THREE:** Build a Community

**CHOICE FOUR:** Listen to Lived Experience Experts

**CHOICE FIVE:** Share What had Lasting Impact

**CHOICE SIX:** Engage with Impact

**CHOICE SEVEN:** Be the Needed Change

**Join the Life Changing Movement at jitfosteryouth.org/100KCommunity**

# APPENIDIX, RESOURCES & STUFF

## Sources for Foster Youth Statistics

**AFCARS Report #29 from Children's Bureau**, An Office of the Administration for Children and Families (U.S. Department of Health & Human Services) FY 2021 Estimates as of June 28, 2022
https://www.acf.hhs.gov/cb/report/afcars-report-29

**American Academy of Pediatrics Website** updated July 21, 2021 Mental and Behavioral Health Needs of Children in Foster Care
https://www.aap.org/en/patient-care/foster-care/mental-and-behavioral-health-needs-of-children-in-foster-care/

**Annie E. Casey Foundation (AECF) website**
Child Welfare and Foster Care Statistics
Updated September 26, 2022
https://www.aecf.org/blog/child-welfare-and-foster-care-statistics

"What the Data Say About Race, Ethnicity and American Youth," Updated September 4, 2020, originally posted June 17, 2018
https://www.aecf.org/blog/what-the-data-say-about-race-ethnicity-and-american-youth

**Center on Juvenile and Criminal Justice**
Justice Policy Journal, Volume 17, Number 2 (Fall 2020)
The Foster-Care-to-Prison Pipeline by Ashly Marie Yamat
http://www.cjcj.org/uploads/cjcj/documents/the_foster_care_to_prison_pipeline.pdf

**Children's Data Network June 6, 2017**
To What Degree Do the Criminal Justice and Child Welfare Populations in California overlap?
https://www.datanetwork.org/news/to-what-degree-do-the-criminal-justice-and-child-welfare-populations-in-california-overlap/

**Finally Family Homes website**
No date on website stats
Christina Dronen, co-founder
https://finallyfamilyhomes.org/the-problem/

**iFoster website** stats updated November 9, 2020
https://www.ifoster.org/blogs/6-quick-statistics-on-the-current-state-of-foster-care/

**The Imprint Youth & Family Newsletter,** "California Leaders Grapple with How to Keep Troubled Youth From Being Sent out of State," by Sara Tiano, March 5, 2021
https://imprintnews.org/child-welfare-2/california-troubled-youth-out-of-state/52488

**National Conference of State Legislatures (NCSL) website** Mental Health and Foster Care November 1, 2019
https://www.ncsl.org/research/human-services/mental-health-and-foster-care.aspx

**National Foster Youth Institute (NFYI) website** "51 Useful Aging Out of Foster Care Statistics/Social Race Media," May 26, 2017 Source: www.nfyi.org/51-useful-aging-out-of-foster-care-statistics-social-race-media/

**Northwest Foster Care Alumni Study** by Harvard Medical School, the University of Michigan, and Casey Family Programs, 2005
https://www.casey.org/media/AlumniStudies_NW_Report_ES.pdf

**Population Reference Bureau (PRB)**
https://www.aecf.org/blog/what-the-data-say-about-race-ethnicity-and-american-youth

**Scientific American,** "How the Pandemic Roiled the Foster Care system," by Carolyn Barber, June 27,2021
https://www.scientificamerican.com/article/how-the-pandemic-roiled-the-foster-care-system/

**Verywell Mind, "**The Mental Health Effect of Living in Foster Care," by Sarah Sheppard February 9, 2022
https://www.verywellmind.com/the-mental-health-effects-of-living-in-foster-care-5216614

**Other References**

**Project Impact Reports** by The Gumpert Foundation, Dialogues In Action, 2016

**Seven Habits of Highly Effective People** by Steven R. Covey, Published by Simon & Schuster, 2020

**Simon Sinek Ted Talk**, 2009
https://www.youtube.com/watch?v=u4ZoJKF_VuA
**The Deepest Well** by Nadine Burke Harris, M.D., Houghton Mifflin Harcourt, 2018

## *Life Changing Choices. Essential Takeaways*

*The American child welfare system is built on assumptions from the 1850's - underlying beliefs, thinking and logic that translate into problem solving which inevitably leads to what would otherwise be judged as unacceptable outcomes today.

*The long-held belief is that "broken" children from "broken homes" should be "placed" outside their communities and "up for adoption."

*These children are often viewed as incorrigible offspring of addicts and lowlifes and some will be further abused in systems that are supposed to protect them.

*Old mental models have led to systems, policies and procedures that encourage aligned behaviors which produce current unhealthy results.

*Instead of being safely reunified with their families — or moved quickly into adoptive homes — many children will languish in foster care for years.

*Suffering from disconnection and a lack of foundational life skills and resources, young people exit the system with dire consequences for themselves and the larger community.

*For any organization seeking to create durable, transformative change, there are **choices to be made** – significant, life-altering choices. The next seven chapters will describe the 7 Essential Choices we faced and made, which we believe were the key to our highly successful impacts.

## Choice One Essential Takeaways: Empower

*When the Choice to Protect is pursued as the central WHY, the only identified Intention, it can constrain and diminish those who are "protected" by avoiding "risky" choices and minimizing growth experiences with limiting, risk-averse policies, procedures, and systems.

*The Choice to Empower embraces the idea that human growth requires trial and error, failures and successes, and the authority to make the decisions that lead to our eventual self-confidence and competence.

*Responsibility and accountability lie with the person being empowered, who also must be understood and armed with the tools to succeed.

*A Theory of Change and Mental Model grounded in Empowerment can serve as the foundational platform for one's services.

*Those served are empowered to succeed and guide the improvement and evolution of the services.

## Choice Two Essential Takeaways: Creative, Resourceful, Whole

*If we see someone as Damaged and Broken, it puts the focus on my role as Rescuer, Fixer, and Savior which may feed my need for significance and being the hero, but it does not support Empowerment, no matter how good my intention might be.

*The Choice to see youth as Creative, Resourceful and Whole is to respect their power and wisdom, recognizing their inner knowledge and capacity to make their own life changing choices at hand.

*Sometimes we may need assistance to access our inner wisdom, which is the benefit of the Just in Time Coach Approach practices: setting aside our agenda, being present, active listening, curious questions, and powerful questions.

*Awareness of Adverse Childhood Experiences (ACEs) helps us change our perspective from "What's wrong with me" to "What happened to me and what can I do to rectify it?"

*Rise to Resilience gives permission for youth with lived experience in foster care to be their authentic selves, openly share their past trauma, understand how it impacts them now, and be empowered to determine how to move forward.

## Choice Three Essential Takeaways: Community

*A System forms a bureaucracy which makes the pieces work together but also builds in constraints on what is allowed and what's possible. Individualization hits the brick wall of risk-averse standardization.

*While a System may appear to be more efficient, the practices are often inflexible and rigid, leaving people out and causing them to feel unsure, disconnected, and unprepared.

*System service providers are fixed in the role of "givers", causing them to experience burnout and compassion fatigue.

*Community sees the interconnectedness of the strengths and needs of each individual; solutions are individualized.

*In Community, young people transform their thinking from believing that life "happens" to them to realizing they can do more than they ever thought possible.

*Community believes individuals are best qualified to lead the discussion on how to address their challenges, with access to caring adults who are there to empower them.

## Choice Four Essential Takeaways: Lived Experience Experts

*"Rescue" is the legacy being carried on by our Child Welfare system today, buoyed by a Bureaucracy that controls and coordinates the elements to work together within a tight web of constraints.

*The "experts" don't make decisions. The Bureaucracy does.

*"We are doing the best we can" becomes an all-too-common justification for results that may not seem optimal for those affected but still fall within acceptable System outcomes.

*Our current and former foster youth are the experts of the foster care experience.

*The Choice to Empower our young people impacted by foster care is an intentional decision to include them in the solution creation process.

*Building Community as an alternative to System/ Bureaucracy is an opportunity to move away from the traditional power positions to consistent inclusion of the voices and choices of the youth and young adults serve

*Participants see themselves as inspirational role models, as exceptional people with bright futures.

## Choice Five Essential Takeaways: Lasting Impact

*Most service organizations set aspirational metrics, and their stakeholders expect that those metrics are being tracked and measured.

*Outputs are Quantitative, tracking "how many and how much," but if outputs don't lead to meaningful change, then they're not useful measurements of progress.

*To measure Qualitative change, it's necessary to go deeper and to assess internal changes: mental, emotional and behavioral shifts.

*We want to track, not just immediate change or benefit, but lasting impact.

*One of the key components to measuring our impacts is asking the right questions and by getting feedback from our participants.

*Overwhelmingly, Alumni surveyed in the JIT Lasting Impact Fulfillment Tracking believed they had broken the cycle of foster care with high levels of satisfaction for well-being.

## Choice Six Essential Takeaways: Sustainability

*Nonprofit emphasis on impacts and mission alignment is fundamental and aligned with meeting financial goals and strategies.

*If you can demonstrate measurable impact, people will be enthusiastic about supporting your efforts.

*A community-based, coach approach fundraising strategy values Impacts and Relationships equally.

*Organizations are like people: they do best when they're connected - to people who care about them and their best interest, who believe in them, and who are committed to their sustainability.

*There needs to be mutual trust between the Board and the Executive Leadership team.

*Outcomes are always better when all board members know their specific role and what they are there to accomplish, with a way to measure their progress and success.

*Use the power of Story and Community.

*Rather than focusing on asking for money, invite the Investor to engage in the mission.

*Extraordinary stewardship: Do the Unexpected.

## Choice Seven Essential Takeaways: Be the Change

*In the beginning, you share your dream with others and persuade them to take a leap into the unknown.

*The middle, as in any good novel or movie, is where most of the tension plays out — the scrappy fight, the steep climb.

*When the dream becomes reality, everyone deserves (and needs) a victory dance. Whether big or small, this "movement" has changed the course of the future.

*<u>YOU</u> can do it! Groups like Fostering Youth Independence and Just in Time for Foster Youth have shown it can be done.